AF655725

MANJU KAPUR

A Postmodern Critical Reading

MANJU KAPUR

A Postmodern Critical Reading

Dr. Premila Swamy D

AUTHORSPRESS

Worldwide Circulation through Authorspress Global Network

First Published in July 2021

by

Authorspress

Q-2A Hauz Khas Enclave, New Delhi-110 016 (India)

Phone: (0) 9818049852

E-mail: authorspressgroup@gmail.com

Website: www.authorspressbooks.com

Manju Kapur: A Postmodern Critical Reading

ISBN 978-93-90891-53-5

Copyright © 2021 Dr. Premila Swamy D

All rights reserved. No part of this book may be reproduced or transmitted in any form or by any means, electronic, mechanical, photocopying, or otherwise, without the express written consent of the author.

Printed in India at Thomson Press (India) Limited

Dedicated to
My Parents

Who spent their lives serving in Vivekananda Kendra Vidyalayas, Arunachal Pradesh and raising us in the remote hills of India's North East

Manju Kapur (1948 -)

Author of *Difficult Daughters* (1998), *A Married Woman* (2000), *Home* (2006), *The Immigrant* (2008), *Custody* (2011), *Brothers* (2016)

Foreword

Dr. V. Sangeetha
Professor & HOD, Department of English, Periyar University, Tamil Nadu

Postmodernism in literary studies is way of reading texts and situating it within the postmodern tendencies and approaches that seek to question and subvert grand narratives. Literary texts become a wide platform to examine oppressive structures and mediate resistance and reorientation of our thoughts usually conditioned by historical metanarratives. In this context, this book offers deep analysis of Manju Kapur's works from a postmodern and postmodern feminist critical school of thoughts. Manju Kapur stands tall in the map of South Asian feminist writers and her works no doubt requires scholarly attention. The present analytical work on Kapur gives insights on gender and identity which in postmodern context are unstable and fluid notions. Considering the tenets set by postmodern thinkers and drawing inferences from discourses led by Michael Foucault, Jacques Derrida, Jean Lyotard, Edward Said, Lucy Iragary, Judith Butler and other philosophical discussions, this work takes a full shape from scholarly thesis to a book form. Diverging from identity politics to gender subjectivities and drawing parallel attention to sexual orientation, this book provides an enriching reading experience of Kapur's works. This book aptly situates Manju Kapur as a postmodern liberal feminist.

The language and diction used is user friendly; the chapters dwell on theoretical frameworks along with texual analysis and within its framework, make a valuable reading for all academicians and researchers engaged in postmodern reading of texts.

Best Wishes!

Sangeetha

Dr. V. SANGEETHA, Ph.D.
Professor & Head
Department of English
Periyar University
Salem 636 011. T.N. India

Preface

Indian English fiction has evolved under the influence of various historical, political and social stages that the country witnessed at different time periods. Indian English fiction has developed not only thematically but also in its form, technique, narrative strategies and the usage of English as a creative expression. If the early novels laid emphasis on social realism and nationalism, the writers of post-independence period wrote about the after effects of partition, urbanisation, East/west cultural conflicts, individual psyche and so on. On the other hand, postmodern fiction concentrated on the idea of celebration or playfulness unlike the modern fiction that resonated elements of despair and disillusionment. Intertextuality, hybridity, turning to history, reinventing and reinterpreting myths and folk narratives, sexual frankness, to caricature the present personalities, to allegorise, to resist patriarchal power structures to subvert the canonical order and question the hegemony, to give voice to the subaltern and deconstruct different ideologies especially the concepts of nation, nationhood and identity are some characteristics that significantly mark postmodern fiction. The substantial growth has led Indian English fiction to receive wide readership and international fame and success. Today, we can note that Indian English fiction is at par with any other literatures of the world.

Manju Kapur is a celebrated contemporary women writer from India and stands tall amongst the South Asian women writers. The book is an analytical and critical interpretation of the works of Manju Kapur, especially from the light of postmodern tendencies.

Deconstruction and postmodern feminist approaches are applied to the study of the texts. The first chapter is an historical survey and a background study of the rise of the Indian English fiction. This chapter is a detailed study on the various historical, political and social aspects that shaped Indian English fiction from the beginning till the contemporary period. It also talks about the growth of Indian women novelists and gives an overview of Manju Kapur as a writer and her thematic concerns. The next chapter discusses in brief the chief tenets of postmodern tendencies and postmodern feminist concerns. The subsequent chapters analyse and situate Manju Kapur as a Postmodern writer by focusing on issues pertaining to identity, gender and sexuality. Systematic interpretation is undertaken in terms of conflicts and resolution as traced in the texts; along with Kapur's narrative art and usage of language. Hence, the book would benefit academicians and scholars to understand the critical discourses under postmodernism and its application in the interpretation of texts. The book gives a fresh understanding of Manju Kapur's work and hence would prove beneficial in situating other Indian writers as well.

Dr. Premila Swamy D

Acknowledgements

This book is a humble effort to compose my doctoral thesis on Manju Kapur into a comprehensive book form. In this process of shaping my thesis into a concrete book form, there are many whose sincere advice and encouragement needs to be placed on record. I take this opportunity to thank all of them.

Firstly, I thank my Professor Dr. S. Venkateswaran, Former Professor & Director, Regional Institute of English, South India, Bangalore for his guidance on my research work and constant encouragement to accomplish this task.

I express my sincere gratitude to Dr. V. Sangeetha, Professor & HoD, Department of English, Periyar University, Tamil Nadu for guiding me with her valuable inputs, suggestions for improvement and writing a foreword for this book.

I am honoured to be surrounded with academic friends who no doubt have been a consistent motivating factor to drive me complete this work. Here, I mention my earnest note of thanks to my friend Dr. Sanjay N Shende, Assistant Professor of English, Shree Shivaji College, Rajura, for his constructive feedback, guidance and support rendered in proof reading this work and its completion within the timeframe.

My institution, M. S. Ramaiah Institution of Technology has always inspired its staff to outshine in academic endeavours. This is an outcome of their encouraging words.

Without the support and cooperation of Authorpress, New Delhi, India, this book would not have been realised. I am sincerely grateful to them in transforming my work into a beautifully designed and readable book.

My heartfelt thanks to my parents, my spouse Shri Mrigendra Goswami, and son Krishanu Goswami for bearing with me patiently and helping me to execute this work in a paced manner.

Lastly, I thank all the readers who have entrusted upon me to get valuable insights from this book.

Dr. Premila Swamy D

Contents

1

The Rise of the Indian English Fiction: Historical Perspective

The most suitable mode of reaching the common masses to deliver a significant thought and social consciousness is no doubt the visual media and in literature, it is fiction and drama, the two genres that have grown as powerful mediums of expression. This is because the audience is able to directly relate to different experiences that one is surrounded with. Literary expressions in India flourish not only in regional languages but also in English which is no longer considered as an alien language. Today, we speak of different 'Englishes': American English, British English, African English, Indian English and so on. English is suitably molded to suite the local flavor and environment, acting as a means of expression to reach a larger audience especially in a multilingual country like India. To enable a better understanding, a historical survey of Indian English writings is essential. The historical and political movement that shaped and accelerated Indians to write in English is discussed as a background study. This chapter identifies some of the chief concerns of the pre-independence, post-independence writings, and postmodern fiction which allows the reader to get a complete grasp of the rise of Indian English fiction to its present stage.

Indian English literature originated primarily due to the impact of British imperialism and colonisation. With the establishment of East India Company and the expansion of Christian missionaries, English education entered the Indian soil. The colonisers came to India for trade and shortly realised that stable political governance would substantially increase their profits. The Industrial Revolution in the eighteenth-century England could only sustain itself through the capital generated in the Indian territories through revenue collection. To enable strong political hold in a multilingual country, the need for a class of people who could act as interpreters between the colonisers and the locals was felt. Thus, came into being the introduction of English education in India. Charles Grant, one of the directors of East India Company, pleaded for the adaption of the English language in 1792. After much debate and resistance, later, after a gap of forty-three years, the English language was adopted in1835 for the promotion of the European literature and science among the natives of India. In the mid-19th century, social reformers like Raja Ram Mohan Roy vociferously supported English education to uproot social evils and also provide new employment opportunities in the administration that required the knowledge of English language. Lord Macaulay, a member of colonial Indian parliament, in his famous minutes' talks about producing "mimic men" through this education system who belong to "a class who may be interpreters between us and the millions who we govern; a class of persons, Indians in blood and colour, but English in taste, in opinions, in morals and in intellect" (35). Macaulay articulated his ideas of western education by making a very derogatory and biased statement that "a single shelf of a good European library was worth the whole native literature of India and Arabia" (14). Initially Indians were skeptical towards English education but later welcomed it. English language brought people from different ethnic groups closer and through literary expressions; they were able to reach a larger audience. But it should be kept in mind that it was only the elite and privileged class who could study in English medium schools and could thus verbalise in English. The educated Indians started experimenting with different literary expressions to articulate their passionate thoughts and feelings. At the initial stage, creative expressions were a direct influence of the western writers and imitating them was the trend. The influence of Romanticism and Romantic writers like Wordsworth, Shelly and Keats is visible in the early writings. Portrayal of landscape and nature represented their key areas of interest. They also wrote about

India's historical past and its heritage. Gradually, Indians started writing in their own style and explored different themes, subsequently resulting in the germination and growth of Indian English literature. Today, Indian English literature has got a prominent place in world literature and Indian writers are widely appreciated and their works have become a part of the academic curricula.

Fiction, through ages whether it is Indian English fiction or fiction written in vernacular medium has depicted the saga of human activities and experiences, emotions, cultural ethos and sentiments. Today, in the era of digital world, we see that technology has taken over all other fields and the visual media has given substantial works connecting with the public. Yet the popularity of fiction in particular and the enthusiasm of the reading public have not come down. The universal popularity of fiction is the way it mirrors life. In its creative process, it gives direct insights on the life and society around us. A fiction becomes a platform for the author to portray the life experiences pertaining to a particular society and the reader in turn is able to connect himself or herself to various experiences revealed thus leaving scope for thought and new perceptions. Robert. B. Henkle rightly states "fiction and drama present men and women reacting to each other in the way that is closer to real life" (1).

Of all the genres in Indian English literature, the novel as a genre was the last to arrive and made a dissident beginning during the nineteenth century India. Story telling is definitely the part of Indian way of life. Indian folk arts, dance forms, legends, the epics and the mythologies are stories naturally, for fiction writers to explore and reinvent. Initially fiction writing was only in the vernacular form. Critic Meenakshi Mukherjee notes "the Indo-Anglian novel came into existence long after the novel had become an established genre in other Indian languages" (18).

Although fiction was the last to emerge, it gradually evolved into great heights and today it has received universal recognition. Prof. M. K. Naik expresses his views about novel writing in India:

> ......one of the notable gifts of English education to India is prose fiction for though India was probably a fountain head of story-telling, the novel as we know today was an importation from the west (99).

As mentioned earlier, the emergence of English education provided by the Christian missionaries in the nineteenth and twentieth century left way for Indians writing in English. The impact of the colonial power is directly felt with the flowering of Indians, experimenting with the language for creative expressions. The novel as a form is described by Meenakshi Mukherjee in *Realism and Reality* as:

> ...the birth and the development of the novel in India 'as genre nursed by, if not born out of tension between opposing systems of values in a colonial society, and modified by certain indigenous pressures (5).

Meenakshi Mukherjee evaluates the early Indian novels thus:

> Inspite of the various limitations and incompatibilities, the novel in India which began under the British tutelage soon acquired its own distinctive character (6).

The works of Bankim Chandra Chatterjee, Sarat Chandra, Raj Lakshmi Debi and Toru Dutt bear testimony to this. The Indian English fiction passed through various stages before it reached the present status. Lord Macaulay's *Minutes* on Indian education in 1935 and Lord Bentinck's decision to promote European literature and science among the Indians instigated Indians to use an alien tongue for creative expression. Inspired by this policy, a few Indians from the English-educated elite classes such as Raja Ram Mohan Roy, Swami Vivekananda, Sri Aurobindo, Rabindranath Tagore, Sarojini Naidu were stimulated to use English for creative expression. They realised that by using English, they could reach pan-India and even the world audience. Thereafter, the Indian writers in English accepted English as a medium of expression for political and cultural reasons. The advent of printing press made possible the establishment and issuing of newspapers and journals in English and Indian languages in an overwhelming manner. This media had created new opportunities for Indians to write, publish and communicate across the country. A major development in Pre-independence period was the rise of Bengal Renaissance – an intellectual and cultural movement in Calcutta, Bengal, which was both the British capital and the nucleus of Bengali culture. The writers of Bengal Renaissance were pioneers who led the way in synthesising Indian and western ideas in literature and culture. Writers like Bakimchandra and Saratchandra Chaterjee caught up in the provincial patriotism, revived the regional languages, giving rise to a new genre of Indian writing in English, initially termed as Indo-Anglican literature. It was with the Bengal literary renaissance that novel writing emerged and later could be seen in educated provinces like Madras and Bombay. The contribution of the Young Bengal movement led by Henry Derozio and his followers laid the foundation of the Bengal Renaissance. This group sparked intellectual awakening in Bengal through literary expressions. The early nineteenth century underwent an intellectual awakening in response to the newly acquired European knowledge in philosophy, history, sciences and literature.

Bakim Chandra Chatterjee, Toru Dutt, Romesh Chandra Dutt, and Rabindranath Tagore and others were the first few upper class Bengali writers who started to explore the newly adopted language for their creative expressions. These writers represented the social issues and used the novel form as a vehicle for social reforms. Bakim Chandra Chatterjee's *Rajmohan's Wife,* which first appeared in a serialised form in 1864 and was posthumously published in book form in 1935, is considered as the first Indian English fiction. Most novels during the nineteenth century were imitative in nature. It is assumed that Indian novel in English has its roots in the nineteenth century realistic tradition of English Novel. During the formative years, the European masterpieces of Leo Tolstoy, Henerie Balzac and Fyodor Dostoevsky in English translations became the bench mark. The impact of the novels of the Romantics and the early Victorian fiction was visible. However, they did not blindly copy them but tried to establish Indian sentiments and cultural heritage through English words. Rabindranth Tagore's masterpiece,

Gora is a patriotic and political novel articulating vigorously the hopes and aspirations of the colonial India. Tagore also highlights the evil practices, particularly the injustices against women and the downtrodden. The literature of this period produced by Indians depicted political consciousness and nationalism. Reinterpretation of India's past cultural heritage and usage of Indian myths and legends in the narratives were evident. Sri Aurobindo is the first Indian English writer who started the re-interpretation of myths.

The impact of English education, rise in national consciousness and the influence of European models are the chief factors responsible for the growth and development of Indian novel in English. The impact of First World War, the national awakening and freedom struggle led by Mahatma Gandhi formed the corpus of the pre-independence fiction. The emergence of the famous trio namely Mulk Raj Anand, R. K. Narayan and Raja Rao in 1930s brought a new dimension to Indian English fiction. These writers are known as 'The Big Three' an epithet coined by notable critic William Walsh. Their fiction was realistic, didactic and had a reformatory message. They were labeled by William Walsh (1990:62) as "the founding fathers", "the genuine novelists" "and inaugurators of the form". They made their appearance in the thirties with the publication of *Untouchable* (1935), *Swami and friends* (1935) and *Kanthapura* (1938) respectively and became the first trend setters. Their focus was to portray the Indian society as it is: oppression, exploitation and the rigid caste system. Narayan's fiction reveals socio-cultural dilemma in the lives the middle-class people. These early writers were often called the first-generation novelists who addressed national and social problems. M.K Naik rightly remarks:

> Indian novel in English around 1930s needed the novelists who could grasp the social scene with an insight into the human consciousness and who could interpret the real world, distinctive in themes, issues and treatment in their fiction (107).

Mulk Raj Anand is a humanist and novelist with a social purpose. Anand himself says that novel is a weapon of humanism.

He has concerns for the down trodden and the lower-class people. He is greatly influenced by Charles Dickens, H.G. Wells and Tolstoy, both in form and characterisation. The ideologies set by western Marxism and Eastern Gandhism has had a visible impact on Anand's works. Human predicament, injustice, human values, status of women, exploitation by class, caste and imperialism form his major themes. Anand's early novels, *Coolie* (1936), *Two Leaves and a Bud* (1937), *Village* (1939), *Across the Black Waters* (1940), *The Sword and the Sickle* (1942) bear testimony to this fact.

R. K. Narayan, on the other hand, is a novelist of middle class sensibility. Narayan is gifted with natural story telling about the southern life style with a touch of wit and humour. The world of Narayan's fiction centres around Malgudi, an imaginary south Indian town as Thomas Hardy invented his Wessex. His usage of simple, plain and realistic English is much admired.

Raja Rao, another distinguished writer of the time, was slightly different from his contemporaries. His concern was largely philosophical and mythological. His first novel *Kanthapura*, a masterpiece of all times is about peasant life and the inflow of Gandhian ideologies in an Indian village. Deeply rooted in metaphysics, some of his other notable works include *The Serpent and the Robe* and *The Cat and Shakespeare: A Tale of India.*

A passionate attraction for the west and a profound love for India were the two regulating factors of this period. The novel and short story – both new forms in Indian writing, had dominated contemporary Indian literature under British influence during the 19th century. Nationalism and the criticism of tyrannical social practices were most favored topics amongst the writers of the period. The novels written during 19th century brought to limelight the social injustices, superstition and the abominable conditions of the peasants and workers. Woman's emancipation, education and widow remarriage also became common themes. In the years between World War I (1914-1918) and World War II (1939-1945), three decisive movements had influenced and stimulated Indian contemporary literature under tremendous British influence and its after-effects. The first was the Non-Violent Movement towards achieving freedom for India, led by Mahatma Gandhi. The others were the international movements of Marxism and Socialism, which had preached better living and working conditions. One can clearly note that the pre-independence writers wrote about freedom struggle, patriotism, Gandhian ideology and its impact on society, social evils like caste system and oppression and the problems of rural India. Realistic representation of the society was the hallmark of the pre-independence novelists.

The post-independence period marked the beginning of Modernism in Indian English Literature. Modernism as a technique and philosophy came to the Indian literary scene only after independence. The world wars brought in the feeling of gloom, despair and alienation which is much reflected in literary output. Literature in English, no doubt, came to maturity and wide acclaim post-independence. The focus was on the impact of partition and after effects, linguistic and communal riots, cross-cultural conflict, east-west encounter, problems under industrialisation and modernisation. The impact of world wars and the philosophies of the western writers were tremendous. On one hand, there was freedom to be celebrated, and on the other hand independence brought the division of the Indian subcontinent into two nations, India and Pakistan – partition followed by severe violence and bloodshed. Much of the Indian fiction after 1947 thus explored, in one way or another, the consequences of partition on Indian culture. Another ongoing concern was the rapid rate of change that India was experiencing in an era of increased globalisation and of the migration of people from the Indian subcontinent to other parts of the world, especially western countries.

The post-independence fiction had their settings or locales in the metropolis or abroad unlike the earlier novels which was only village centric. The modern novels broadened not only in its setting and thematic range but also experimented with form, technique and language. Post-independence, Modernism and its concepts played a prominent role in shaping the second-generation novelists of the era. The impact of Modernism is seen in notable novelist of the time namely; Bhabhani Bhattacharya, B. Rajan, Malgonkar, Khushwant Singh, Chamal Nahal, Arun Joshi, Kamala Markandaya, Ruth Prawar Jhabwala, Nayantara Sahgal, Anita Desai, Shashi Deshpande and few others. Before independence, the focus was on social, political and historical aspects. Post independent novels were successful in not only depicting the social life but also portraying the individual self. The society and the individual, both were important to these writers. The primary concern of the novelists of 1950s, 60s and the 70s era is the after effects of partition, communal and linguistic riots, impacts of industrialisation and westernisation, social evils, and the exploration of man-woman relationships. Another most significant feature of the post-Independence novels produced during the period between 1950s and 1980s was a shift of emphasis from the external to the internal, the socio-political issues to the individual problems. Anita Desai and Arun Joshi carved out a niche for themselves by dealing with individual problems. Existential issues such as quest for identity, alienation, rootlessness, disillusionment and human predicament were the basic themes. One significant school of thought which inspired the modern writers is the psychological philosophies led by Freud and the ideologies of Existentialism. Both these schools concentrated on the inner psyche of human beings. Psychoanalytical theories of self, devaluation of self, neurosis, sexual repression and nausea given by Dr Karen Horney in *Neorosis and Human Growth* (1953-1957), and Freud in *Life and Works of Sigmund Freud* (1953-1957) published in three volumes, impacted greatly on the post-independence writers such as Anita Desai, Shashi Deshpande, Bharati Mukherjee, Kamala Das, Kiran Desai and few others. Hence in some of the modern novels, written under the influence of this philosophy do not have too many characters but had minimal characters and the story moved in the stream of consciousness technique. The impact of the world wars and modernist notions of life such as disillusionment, alienation, loneliness, restlessness and despair at the prevalent situation was clearly reflected in European writers. In the Indian context, for writers like Arun Joshi and Anita Desai, the central focus was the individual rather than the society. The theme of alienation, self-pity and escapism are prevalent in the works of Arun Joshi and Chamal Nahal. Search for identity is also the chief concern of novelists like Anita Desai, Kamala Markhandaya, Arun Joshi and many others. The feeling of rootlessness and existentialism is vividly portrayed in B. Rajan's *The Dark Dancer, Too Long in the West,* Santha Rama Rau's *Remember in the House*, Attia Husain's *Sunlight on a Broken Column*, Kamala Markhandaya's *Some Inner Fury* and Anita Desia's *Cry, the Peacock.* Another dominant theme of the post-independence era is the dichotomy between east and west encounters and related cross-cultural issues. Bhattacharya's *Shadow from Ladakh* and Markandaya's *The Coffer Dam* and *Pleasure City* deal with this east/west conflict. Novels written from the psychological aspect are B. Rajan's *The Dark Dancer*, Markandaya's *Silence of Desire* and most of the novels of Arun Joshi and Anita Desai. The influence of Freudian philosophy and the writings of Virginia Woolf left great impact on these writers.

There is a clear shift from the rural and downtrodden to the lives of urban middle class. The locales in the fictional scene shifted from the village to the urban metropolis and also to overseas. Aftermaths of partition, communal riots, alienation, workings of the mind, loneliness and the search for identity were key concerns in the writings after independence. The novelists during the 1950s and 60s got preoccupied with character development. So, there was a shift from society to the individual. The trend of social realism, which flowered in the pre-independence Indian English novels, has been successfully and powerfully continued in the post-independence period by Bhabani Bhattacharya, Manohar Malgonkar and Khushwant Singh, who made their appearance during the 1950s. By the end of the Sixties and in the early Seventies, writers whom we call as postmodern writers addressed issues like globalisation and subsequent multiculturalism. East-west conflict, social realism, gender issues, comic aspect of human nature, ecological concerns, magic realism, and diasporic writings became the themes of the postmodern writers. A significant development in Indian literature during the mid and late 20th

century was the rise of female writers and feminist writing. The emergence of women novelist had a significant impact on the growth of Indian English fiction. The shift in attitude towards women in the wake of feminist movement proved a boon to the fair sex. Post-independence novelists voiced for the status of woman and her identity. Women writers like Kamala Markhandaya, Nayantara Sahgal and Anita Desai engaged themselvcs with issues of women in conventional marriage systems, the patriarchal family circle, human relationships and social and political upheavals.

Indian English fiction witnessed a phenomenal growth during the 1980s. K. R. S Iyengar has rightly pointed that the novel is

> a living and evolving literary genre, and is trying, in the hands of its practitioners, a fusion of form, substance and expression that is recognisably Indian yet also bearing the marks of universality (322).

This statement is valid as we see the different genres within the novel genre outnumbering in the postmodern era. The present era has seen novels like political novels, social novels, magic realism, surrealism, satire, etc.

Indian English writing witnessed a literary renaissance in the 1980s. A major landmark in the history of Indian English fiction is with the publication of *Midnight's Children* in 1981 by Salman Rushdie. Because the impact is so large that sometimes critics tend to bifurcate as Pre Rushdian and Post Rushdian novels. The appearance of *Midnight's Children* brought about a renaissance in Indian writing in English as a whole. Its influence, acknowledged by critics and novelists alike, has been apparent in numerous ways: the appearance of a certain post-modern playfulness, the turn to history, a new exuberance of language, the reinvention of allegory, and the sexual frankness – all seem to appear in the contemporary writers. The trend of magic realism initiated by Rushdie was continued by novelists like Amitav Ghosh and Gita Hariharan. However, the tradition of social realism continued. Social issues like class conflict, gender discrimination, the rich poor divide, caste system, impact of industrialisation, conflict between modern scientific growth and traditional moral values, religious malpractices and superstitions versus scientific progress have also been highlighted. In post 1980 era, love, sex and marriage or the failure of it are some of the leading themes. Frank, unconventional and bold attempts in portraying man – woman relationship in marriage is clearly seen in Shiv K. Kumar's *A River with Three Banks* and Vikram Seth's *A Suitable Boy*. Technically, the post-independent Indian English novelists exhibit a tendency for experimentation in technique and style. The most recurrent narrative technique has been that of the first person point of view. The use of the images, symbols and myths from scriptures and epics is a major aspect of these novels. The two cultural and literary events that shaped its history were: Edward Said's theoretical deliberations in *Orientalism* and the publication of Salman Rushdie's *Midnight's Children* which was a complete departure from the realistic style of representation followed since 1930s. *Midnight's Children* is perhaps the most outstanding and 'ground breaking' novel of this period. It is a multifaceted narrative; it is, at once, an autobiographical bildungsroman, a picaresque comedy, a surrealist fantasy, a political allegory, a political satire and a stylistic experiment. The author describes it as 'sort of modern fairy tale' and the work is an existing blend of natural and the supernatural, political allegory and ethical implications. This epoch-making work brought in new dimension and fresh insights in the literary framework. Postmodern texts do have the negativity of despair and disillusionment; but, they rather tend to celebrate the same occasion in a playful way. Turning to history, postmodern playfulness, sexual frankness, exuberance in language and bold attempts mark the advent of the new age in the literary history. These new generation writers revisit history, history becomes a text in their novels and thus they become historiographers. They bring to the forefront subjects untold and undiscovered, revert to history to find its relevance to the contemporary, to caricature the present personalities, to allegorise, to subvert the canonical order and question the hegemony, to give voice to the subaltern and deconstruct different ideologies especially the concepts of nation, nationhood and identity. Shashi Tharoor's

The Great Indian Novel and Amitav Ghosh's *Calcutta Chromosome* bear these said characteristics. Reinterpretation of myths, legends and legendary figures gives scope for a fresh look and these play a dominant role in the writings of Shashi Deshpande, Gita Hariharan and many others. Some of the writers resist the idea of unity of place in their novels. For example, Vikram Seth sets the scene of his *The Golden Gate* in the U.S.A and in *An Equal Music,* the European countries. In Amitav Ghosh's *The Circle of Reasons* and *The Glass Palace,* the actions take place in India, the U.S.A, Burma and Egypt. Hence, the Aristotelian concept of unity of time, place and action is reversed. The traditional linear mode of narration gives way to dismantled and zigzag form of narration and the narratives fluctuate to various locations and therefore have global characters. The writers of this period broadened their horizons. The philosophical school of Post-structuralism and Deconstruction had a significant impact on these writers. To decentre the centre and question the binary oppositions, they advocate intertextuality; challenge patriarchal and colonial power structures. A significant characteristic of this period is the carefree playfulness with respect to language. Unlike the novelists of the 1930s, they were not conscious in the use of English language. Using Indian idiom and phrases, expressions, coining new words, code switching and code mixing is easily opted to display Indian sensibility, ethos and Indian identity. One best example could be Arundhati Roy's *The God of Small Things*. The novels of this period celebrate multiculturalism and hybridity, recognise multiple identities but resist, decolonise and dismantle hegemonic power structures. Some of the writers who shot into prominence after 1980s are: Vikram Seth, Bharathi Mukherjee, Upamanyu Chatterjee, Amitav Ghose, Gita Mehta, Shoba De, Arundhati Roy, Shashi Deshpande, Salman Rushdie, Vikram Chandra, Rohinton Mistry, Gita Hariharan, Manju Kapur, Jhumpa Lahiri, Kiran Desai and many more. There came about some novelist like Pratap Sharma and Ranga Rao who were interested in the lives and experiences of minorities in India. Thus, fiction writing after 1980s took full shape and became a means of global expression and choice.

English language in the hands of Indian writers took a new form, resulting in the creation of Indian English idiom or diction. During the 80s, the novel flourished and advanced in themes, techniques and use of language. Today, we have postmodern and postcolonial fiction that leaves ample scope for literary interpretation. The international literary awards like The Booker, The Pulitzer, The Sinclair won by Indian novelists exemplify the fact that Indian writers have been recognised by the western counterpart.

There need to be a mention of the different controversies over the nomenclature of the Indian English Literature. From the historical perspective, Indian English literature has passed through several phases such as Indo-Anglican literature, Indo-English literature, Indian Writing in English and recently Indian English literature. This debate came to an end with the publication of *Indian Writing in English* by K. R. Srinivasa Iyengar in 1962. Now, Indian English literature has gained worldwide popularity and is a part of Commonwealth Literatures and Post-Colonial studies. English had definitely brought in a pan Indian consciousness. Postmodern writers engaged themselves with theories on deconstruction, postcolonial and feminist ideologies, indulged in fragmentation, magic realism, plurality, multiculturalism, depiction of subaltern issues, issues of subjectivity and identity, intertextuality, humour and cosmopolitanism.

In this context, the views of R.K. Dhawan validate the flowering of Indian English writing thus:

> It is the present which paves way for the future. The hope for the flourishing of literature in the centuries to come rests on the premise that it is the offshoot or the growth of the twentieth century writing. A number of twentieth century writers have consolidated and given a new turn to Indian writing and thought (9).

There is another class of writers whom we call as Diaspora writers who have chosen to live in abroad and write about their experiences. Some consciously chose to settle in abroad and write from there and some because of their ancestor's settlement over there. These writers are referred as Expatriate or Diaspora writers who majorly talk about their immigrant experiences, displacement, identity crisis, sense of hybridity and a sense of belonging to their home country. Cultural clash and the dichotomy of being caught between two cultures, the east and the west dichotomy become the prominent themes of these writers. To this genre of literature, belong writers like Salman Rushdie, Amitav Ghosh, Vikram Seth, Vikram Chandra, Anita Desai, Bharati Mukherjee, Kiran Desai, Jhumpa Lahiri, Chitra Devkaruni and many more.

Postmodern fiction celebrates multiculturalism and hybridity. Issues of identity, globalisation, westernisation, diaspora sensibility, consumerism, commodification, BPOs, upward mobility and consequent erosion of ethical values are some of the thematic concerns. Critical theories like feminism and post colonialism voiced for the minority groups, marginalised and the oppressed. This led to subaltern and Dalit literature along with the feminist writings. With the advent of new critical theories, issues like otherness, quest for identity and self-definition, the problems of exile and displacement, the agony of alienation and issues of racism were questioned. Postcolonial theory raises discussions with respect to migration, slavery, suppression, resistance, representation, gender, identity, race and ethnicity. In 1970s, it gained prominence perhaps with Edward Said's influential critique of western constructions of the orient in his book, *Orientalism* (1978). Present literature addresses these issues and it is noticed that there is a rise in Diaspora, Subaltern and Dalit literature and also various other forms of feminism like the emergence of 'black feminism'. Indian English literature is no exception to this perspective. Another important aspect to note is the growth of the Subaltern literatures. Many writers have voiced the issues concerning the Dalits and the marginalised group. One such prolific writer was Mahasweta Devi. Her works primarily dealt with the oppressed lives of the tribal community and concern for the minorities.

To sum up, the period after 1980s is a landmark in the history of Indian English fiction as Indian English literature started to receive international fame and recognition. Post-Independence, fiction has given a large scope for creative writers to explore various themes, discourses, techniques combined with experimentation with language. V. S. Naipaul, Nirad C. Choudhury, Shashi Tharoor, Vikram Seth, Rohinton Mistry, Chitra Banerjee Divakaruni, Upamanyu Chatterjee, Jhumpa Lahiri, Amit Choudhury to name a few have lured the readers and academia across the world depicting postcolonial sensibilities. Indian writers are now writing with new zeal and confidence by blending various aspects in their creative expressions. In the present context, we have different genres under the novel form. The novels of magic realism, psychological novels, children's fiction, mystery novels, science fiction and the novels of social realism have all evolved in the present time.

Summing up

Historical Overview of the Indian English Fiction		
Colonisation/ Imperialism	Educational reforms/work of missionaries, reception of Eng language literature by Upper class Indians	1835-Macaulay's minute and education policy
	Advent of Printing press	Print revolution and circulation of books, *Rajmohan's Wife* in 1864
	Bengal Renaissance	Hindu college – Henry Derozio
1920s/30s National movement	Rise of Nationalist/Patriotic literature, Political consciousness	Gandhian influence
	Indian Independence – 1947	Partition
	Rise of the Big Three	Raja Rao, Mulk Raj Anand, R. K. Narayan
	Novels make their presence to global scenario	Reaching to global audience

	Existentialist novels	Stream of consciousness technique, rise of women writers
1980s Global movement	Rise of Salman Rushdie	1980's, Publication of *Midnights's Children*, opens up the international market
	Naturalise and Indianise English	Hybridisation & Chutnification Rushdie as poster face of Indian writing in English
	Experimentation with language and form, narrative patterns	
	Narratives of the nation	Retelling and reinterpreting history
	New studies in literature/Postmodernism/postcolonial	Subaltern studies Dalit writings New feminism

1.1 Women writers in Indian English Fiction

The contribution of women writers to the field of Indian English fiction is noteworthy. The first name that comes to our mind is Kamala Markhandaya. Though born in India, she had spent much of her life in England. Her main concern is east/west encounter and the plight of the downtrodden and women. Her characters' range from the poor peasant society in *Nectar in Sieve*, to the urban population in *A Handful of Rice* and then again moving to the upper class in *The Golden Honey Comb*. Her major themes are urbanisation and the impact of westernisation, the Indian diaspora, cultural conflicts and east/west encounters.

Nayantara Sahgal is a writer who writes from the political aspect. Being the daughter of Vijayalaxmi Pandit and neice of Pt. Jawaharlal Nehru, politics seems to be a natural material for her thematic concerns. Her novels display an array of her close acquaintance with political leaders and national events which form the major plot in all of her novels. The life of the elite class, their hypocrisy and shallow values are beautifully narrated. Her concerns are Indian heritage, values and ethics, condition of women in patriarchal system and the political agenda. Her novels like *A Time to be Happy, Rich like Us, Plans for Departure, Mistaken Identity* talk about identity, east/west conflicts and loss of values at length.

Ruth Prawer Jhabwala, a novelist of European origin talks of cultural conflicts, family and arranged marriage system of India and romantic love. Influence of Jane Austen is evident in her fiction. *To Whom She Will* and *Heat and Dust* are notable works of Jhabwala.

If Kamala Markandaya depicts the social circumstances, Nayantara Sahgal probes into the political domain. We have Anita Desai, who dwells herself into exploring the workings of the mind of her characters, especially women. For Desai, the mystery of the mind is much interesting than the political and social realities. Desai's canvas is the upper-class women who have freedom and luxury, yet they suffer neurosis or mental disorder emerging from lack of emotional support and fulfillment of life. Her concerns are marital discords, man-woman relationship, westernisation, immigration, east/west dichotomies and the representation of inner turmoil in the life of her characters. Preoccupation with existentialism and the metaphysical problems expressed through neurotic, fragile and introvert characters form the base of most of her novels.

Shashi Despande, another leading novelist of the contemporary times deals with urban middle class sensibilities. Her novels *The Dark holds no Terror*, *Roots and Shadow*, *The Binding Vine*, *Small Remedies* highlight the various issues operating in the families and the society of the middle-class families and their consciousness. She concentrates on the lives of Indian women who are fragile and confused at the beginning but as her novels progress, they become assertive, self-realisation takes place and they have better control on their lives.

Bharathi Mukherjee, an Indian born American writer is chiefly concerned with issues pertaining to the idea of identity in a world of hybridity and multiplicity. These issues operate in almost all her novels like *Leave It to Me*, *Desirable Daughters*, and the *The Tree bride*.

Gita Hariharan is more interested in form and technique. She makes ample use of folk tales, myths, legends and oral narrative art to retell and reinvent from a postmodern perspective. For her, ancient texts are not closed texts but leave scope for ample interpretation and retelling in the narrative. Her first novel, *The Thousand Faces of Night* (1992) won the Commonwealth Writers' Prize for best first book in 1993. Her other novels include *The Ghosts of Vasu Master* (1994), *When Dreams Travel* (1999), *In Times of Siege* (2003), and *Fugitive Histories* (2009). Githa Hariharan is also known for her social activism and her concern for women. In 1995, she challenged the Hindu Minority and Guardianship Act as discriminative in the Supreme Court of India and was accorded victory.

Anita Desai's works are particularly known for exploring the inner lives of men and women. Her oeuvre has covered themes such women's oppression, quest for identity, family relationships and the nexus between tradition and modernity. Her novels are rich with visual images and details. Desai weaves together identity politics and gender issues with subtle use of imagery and symbols in most her compositions like *Cry, the Peacock*, *Voices in the City*, *Fire on the Mountain*, *In Custody* and so on.

Arundhati Roy explores myths and tradition, uses history and experiments with language. Her Man Booker prize winning novel *The God of Small things* in 1997 brings to the forefront, issues related to identity, gender, social discrimination and makes free and bold expressions on sex. She is known for making exuberant use of language, coining new words and narrating in a zigzag form. She is admired for brilliant use of language and bold expressions. She is also a political and social activist.

Concern for the various aspects of a woman's life becomes the basic theme of most of the women writers. Some of the common themes of the women writers in general are: Gender discrimination and the related problems in a patriarchal society, the issue of identity, cultural conflicts and conflicts in human relationships. Issues pertaining to traditional Indian culture, female education, quest for cultural roots, the east/west confrontation, social injustices, Psychological and existential crises, the clash between tradition and modernity are some thematic concerns of these writers.

Thus, twentieth century witnessed the arrival of many new woman writers whose works mark a significant contribution. According to Susie Tharu:

> These writers contested the structures that were shaping their world. They tactically redeployed dominant discourses, held on to older strains, and recharged them with new meanings and even introduced new issues, new emphasis, new orientations (154).

1.2. Manju Kapur: An Overview

Manju Kapur is a prolific novelist of the contemporary period. She was born in 1948 in Amritsar, in the northern state of Punjab. She pursued her under graduation from Miranda House, Delhi University. She received an M. A in English in 1972 from Dalhouise University, Halifax in Canada and later did an M. Phil from Delhi University. She has opted to leave teaching to devote time to her writings. She was initially an academician and also a writer. She taught English literature in Miranda House College, Delhi University for over 25 years under the name Manju Kapur Dalmia. She is married to Gun Nidhi Dalmia; they have three children and three grandchildren and live in New Delhi.

Manju Kapur is one of the notable writers among South Asian writers. Her first novel, *Difficult Daughters* published in 1998, won the Commonwealth Prize for the best first novel, Eurasia region. Manju Kapur's fiction shows that she has a serious concern for the problems faced by men and women in different walks of life. Deconstructing certain ideologies, resistance to patriarchal power structures, usage of history, issues operating within a family structure, sexual frankness and bold attempts, mark Kapur's fiction.

Some of the striking narrative strategies adopted by Kapur in her novels are: use of history, role of memory, flashback technique, and abundant use of food imagery, use of sensual images, using letters and diary form, multiple perspectives, shift of locales, code switching and code mixing.

Kapur started her writing career at the age of 42. She has written six fictions till date. Her first novel, *Difficult Daughters* published in 1998, won the Commonwealth Prize for the best first novel, Eurasia region. Her second novel, *A Married Woman* published in 2002 was shortlisted for the Encore Award; her third, *Home* in 2006, was shortlisted for the Hutch-Crossword prize, and the fourth *The Immigrant*, in 2008 was short listed for the India Plaza Golden Quill Award, and the DSC prize of South Asian Literature in 2010. She has also edited *Shaping the World: Women Writers on Themselves*, 2014. Her fifth novel *Custody*, published in 2011 has been serialised for soap operas in many regional languages. It has been the basis of *Yeh Hai Mohabbatein,* a daily serial telecasted on Star plus under Ekta Kapur's production house Balaji Telefilms. Soap Operas like *Pranayam* in Malayalam, *Kalyanam Mudhal Kadhal Varai* in Tamil, *Avanu Mathe Shravani* in Kannada, *Mon Niye Kachakachi* in Bengali have all been produced based on Kapur's fifth novel *Custody.* Her recent novel, *Brothers* got published in 2016.

Kapur's thematic concerns are domestic life of middle class educated women, extra-marital affairs, alienation, search for identity, gender discrimination, concern for the girl child, social evils, traditions and values, family system and bindings, infertility, sexual harassment, love and longing, issues related to immigration, middle class sentiments, patriarchy, role of education in emancipation of women, emergence of New Women and so on. Her novels are serious in concern, making it more thought provoking. Kapur's fiction stresses on the woman's need for self-realisation. Her new generation of women characters is bold, assertive, and independent and defies traditional roles imposed on them. They react to situations more independently and can make bold decisions. Self-realisation and introspection paved way for growth from silent, enduring women to someone who is independent in her thought processes. She attempts to portray Indian women who try to break the male hegemony and realise their own self. Kapur emphatically puts all these in her works working close to everyday men and women that she sees. Hence, she uses traditional linear narrative technique and a language that is simple to comprehend to reach to larger audiences. Her ample use of regional expressions makes Indian readers attach themselves with the characters of the novel to easily relate to life and situations. Social realism forms the hallmark of her fiction. She blends English, Hindi and Punjabi words to give realistic touch. Her novels are full of instances of Indianisation of vocabulary, loan translation, use of repetition and linguistic creativity. The narratives of Indian History like the partition, Babri Masjid issue, the Emergency period etc. are interwoven into the main plot. India's past becomes a backdrop in most of her fiction on which the story unfolds. The problematics of nation and history, of gender and identity are skillfully woven into the main story line.

Difficult Daughters (1998), Kapur's first fiction deals with three generations of women against the backdrop of India's freedom struggle and its attainment. Located primarily in the India of the 1940's Manju Kapur speaks of the idea of independence – independence aspired to and obtained by a nation and also independence yearned after by a woman. The novel movingly evokes the multiple frustrations encountered by the central character, Virmati, in her efforts to educate herself and establish a domestic space. While Kasturi, her mother is confined to child bearing and domestic work, the generation of Virmati took some bold and radical steps in joining the political movement for India's freedom, asserted the need for woman's education and independence. Virmati's daughter Ida is the narrator who represents the third generation of women who is much more assertive in her decisions. Bhagpat Nayak rightly observes about different themes in *Difficult Daughters*:

> *Difficult Daughters* presents larger issues of patriarchy, which denies woman's voice and freedom set around at the time of partition.
>
> .... the novelist expresses her absorbing ideas of woman relationship, woman sexuality, love, infatuation, jealousy, marriage, gender roles, self-discovery, and other problems with intelligence and sympathy (209).

A Married Woman (2000), Kapur's second novel is the story of a married woman who finds love and friendship and emotional fulfillment in a same sex relationship set against the Babri Masjid – Ram Janmabhoomi issue. The novel is a kind of narrative on a woman's incompatible marriage and resultant frustration and contemporary political turmoil in its historical context. Kapur in this novel, stresses on the complex portrayal of the social and communal unrest. The focus here shifts from a woman's rebellion against society shackled in traditions, torn between duty and desire, to an exploration of the positioning of women in sexual orientation. With women as its central theme once again, Kapur raises the question of identity which has been related to the representations of lesbians in literature and culture. It is not altogether a novel about lesbian relationship, but rather pointing at a small segment of an unfulfilled longing and love, sort out in a companionship with other women. The central character namely Astha's growing discontent and dissatisfaction is shown against a background of Indian political and social unrest. Thus, the novel explores Astha's longing for a purpose of her life and her desire to assert her individualism through her struggle between two worlds – the heterosexual world she opts for and the lesbian world she enjoys which is more an incidental happening resulting from her predicament not an outcome of sexual desire. Blending the personal with the external, Kapur beautifully entwined the major historical event with the lives of her characters and depicts the political situation with the same fervor and graphic detail as she describes the protagonist Astha's turmoil. The novel explicitly presents two controversial subjects: Hindu-Muslim confrontation and same sex intimacy. According to Sunita Sinha:

> Kapur's novel explores the twin explosive subjects of sexual intimacy between women and Hindu Muslim confrontation against a backdrop of respectable middle class Delhi life (165).

Home (2006), Manju Kapur's next novel, explores the lives of ordinary middle-class women in a joint family system. The novel depicts three generations of an Indian family involved in a family business and talks about their lives, family values and traditions. The novel has a period ranging from the mid-60s to near present. It presents before us a traditional joint family of shopkeepers where women are destined to be married off and are only expected to be a good wife and mother. The lives of three generations of men and women revolve around the Banwarilal cloth shop. The shop set by the patriarch of the family, Lala Banwarilal who had once stood against in the ways of modernisation is carried on by the next generation. The second half of the book revolves on the character Nisha, her trials and tribulations and her struggle to establish herself. Women are the major victims of tradition and orthodoxy. According to Anupama Chowdhury "Home reveals a disturbing home truth that joins families can both destroy and preserve our maturity, individuality and mental progress" (33).

The Immigrant (2008) is an attempt to explore the concepts of migration, dislocation, displacement and cultural identity, and explore the sensibilities of the Indian diasporic community. Kapur's *The Immigrant* has very minimal characters unlike her other novels. The novel revolves around the central character Nina, who at a late age is married to Ananda, a NRI settled in Canada as a dentist and her life in a foreign country. She is into a constant negotiation with her life as a married woman and her adjustment to a new land. The story unfolds in how she adopts and adapts to a new culture with an initial fear and resistance to her new world. She gradually learns to assert her individuality and enjoys freedom. Nina and Ananda and his uncle represent the Indian diasporic community. Kapur's concerns are for the Indian emigrants who face different challenges in adjusting to a new environment. Kapur shows the complexity in life of a newly wed Indian woman through the protagonist Nina. Issues of identity, of being in 'in-betweenness', confrontations with racism, nostalgia for the homeland, cultural clash, double identity, of being 'othered' and the theme of individuality are the aspects dealt with as the story moves ahead with different episodes. Anupama Chowdhuri comments:

> Socio-political problems of contemporary life portrayed in terms of individual's quest for identity and freedom along with a sensitive handling of issues like gender, sexuality and diasporas make The Immigrant a novel with a difference (41).

Custody (2011), Kapur's fifth novel is a moving story of marriage discord, divorce and its impact on young children. The familial binding and man-woman relationship and the harmful effects of ego clashes and maladjustments in married life are vividly portrayed. In *Custody,* some of the themes she deals with are man-woman relationship, infertility, sexuality, beauty, education and divorce. However, Kapur makes effort not to be confined to issues only about women. Raman's experience of divorce and the question of custody of his children are intricately and movingly narrated. A slight deviation is noticed in the sense that Kapur shows the anguish, frustration and anger at the betrayal Raman experiences at the hands of his worldly wife. This novel shows author's concern for the suffering man and the woman in an unsuccessful marital relationship and its impact on the psyche of children.

Brothers (2016) Kapur's recent novel is a family saga that narrates back and forth tracing three generations of a Jat family in Lalbanga, near Ajmer. The story of Tapti Gaina is intimately linked with the lives of two brothers, in a narrative that spans eighty years. The story has its backdrop; World War II, Freedom struggle, the Post-Independence period, through the Emergency and then enters 2010. The movement of the family from rural to urban landscape and their gradual rise from landlords to political masters forms the plot of the tale. Along with, Kapur weaves together caste politics, subordination of women and empowerment through education. Marginalisation and victimisation under oppressive structures forms the quintessential essence of the novel.

Manju Kapur's fiction thus shows that she has a serious concern for the problems faced by men and women in different walks of life. She presents before us a detailed picture of the existing society using a realistic approach. In the chapters to follow, the key concerns from the perspective of Postmodern, Postcolonial and Deconstructive discourses are discussed.

2

Postmodern Tendencies

2.1 Postmodernism

Postmodernism refers to changes, developments and tendencies which have taken/are taking place in literature, art, music, architecture, philosophy and other arts since 1980s. Postmodernism is a historical and cultural tendency and a dominant practice of the 20th century. Many theorists have tried to place this term within a single framework, though postmodernism cannot be limited to a single definition. It defies the conventional, ordinary practions and celebrates non-linear events. Postmodernism is an attitude of rejection towards grand narratives and ideologies that regulates and maintains power. Postmodern thought is governed by tendencies such as self-consciousness, morality, truth and pluralism. Postmodern critical approaches took a phenomenon turn in the 1980s and1990s and have become part of academic and theoretical disciplines like cultural studies, linguistics, feminist theory and literary criticism. It is often associated with schools of thought such as Deconstruction and Post-structuralism. Major postmodern thinkers include Jacques Derrida, Michael Foucault, Jean-Francois Lyotard, Fredric Jameson and Judith Butler. The main proponents include: rejection of binary oppositions, hierarchies, stable identity and categorisation. Postmodernism can be associated with the power shifts and dehumanisation of the post-Second World War era and the onslaught of consumer capitalism. It represents a shift in perception. It rejects rigid boundaries and embraces plurality in form, meaning and identity.

Postmodernism is not an organised movement. It is slippery in nature and hence cannot be fit in one framework for classification.

It celebrates chaos in a playful way, rejects lament and celebrates fragmentation. It has embracing attitude. Some very postmodern texts are; *Slaughter House Five*, or *Children's Crusade: A Duty*, *If on a winter's night a traveller* etc. Modernist writing had lot of seriousness, gravity and laments over loss but Postmodernism celebrates it with a playful attitude. There is deliberate employment of unrealiable narrator in fictions. We notice a shift in attitude. Continuous struggle for wholeness and unity as seen in modernist writing is differed and no conventional sense of beginning, middle and end is held in the narrative pattern. There is blurring of boundaries, preference for fragmentation and fascination with the strategies of representation. There is desire for flows, multiplicities, process rather than order, organisation and tyrannical coherence. Samuel Becket's *Waiting for Godot* talks about the postmodern condition without lamenting and rather celebrating in a humourous way. Modernist writers engaged with fragmented reality, loss of the past and tradition. For eg. James Joyes's Novel *Ulysses*, Yeats's *Second Coming* and Eliot's *The Wasteland* (a heap of broken images). Modernism and Postmodernism both engaged with fragmented reality, it is in postmodernism that we see a celebration of fragmentation.

Post-structuralism and Deconstruction have close connection with postmodernism. Foucault, Barthes, Derrida, Lyotard and Kristeva are postructuralists who deal with language and text. Lyotard talks about grand narratives/meta-narratives like Marxism, Christianity and says that the meta-narratives are created and reinforced by power structures and hence they are also untrustworthy. Deconstruction is an offshoot of postructuralism. Its pioneer, Jacques Derrida goes against totalitarianism and certainity of meaning. According to him, a text is embedded with meaning and therefore leaves scope for multiple readings. It encourages a kind of reading which would bring the layers of constructed meaning. Thus, the reader engages in meaning making process, moving away from a single idea of truth. Derrida talks about difference of meaning where every signifier refers to other words/signifiers and generates multiple meanings. This is suggestive of alternative ways of reading and understanding of a given text. Deconstruction school of thought rejects logo centric attitude, binaries and hierarchies. Derrida talks about the textuality of text where there is a constant engagement with the process of reading in meaning generation. This is undecidability nature of text.

Therefore, in postmodern discourse, text becomes a platform for meaning making process. Through reading, readers get engaged in meaning making process and hence text cannot offer fixity of meaning. Postmodern thinkers like Derrida postulated that there is nothing outside the text and text leaves gaps for multiple interpretations. Also, one text can relate to other texts, there are inferences to other texts in postmodern writing. This idea of textuality of text or intertextuality is put forward by Julia Kristeva in 1960s. Even in terms of narration, there is no one single reliable narrator. The concept of willing suspension of belief so much celebrated in Victorian times is deferred. In fact, there is a conscious fact that it is a story. In postmodern context, everything is considered unstable, flowing, multidimensional and not fixed. The ideas put forward in terms of gender, text or identity reflect this. How things get constructed and represented are the dictums of postmodern writings. Subversion and alternative ways of writing, resistance and debunking the grand narratives like patriarchal power structure are some of the notions that one can come across.

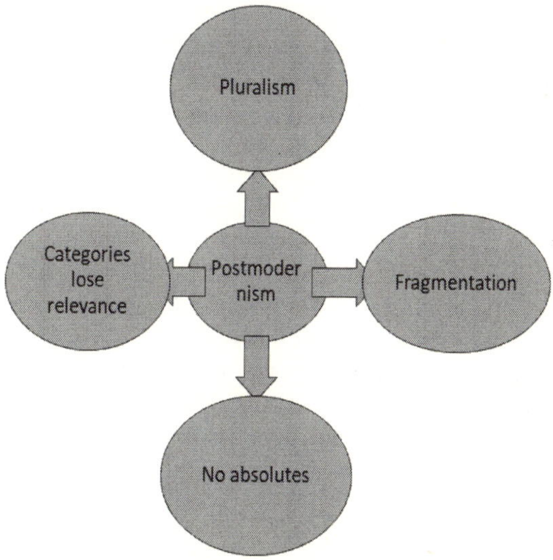

Figure 1 Shows the Main Postulates of Postmodernism

2.3 Postmodern Tendencies

Postcolonial and postmodern literary writings focus on how things get represented/ misrepresented or not get represented in the main stream narratives. Contemporary writing involves in deconstructing the grand narratives, hegemonic canons and aim to re-establish the existing codes laid by power structures that hold, control and regulate these discourses to sustain its order. Literature becomes a means to revisit and deconstruct and reconstruct the established power structures. These writers use literature as a medium to subvert and challenge received perceptions and thereby sensitise and generate awareness. Literature acts as a tool for critiquing social disparities, to show resentment and also for self-exploration and expression.

Postmodernism in literature is characterised by the use of metafiction, self-reflexivity, unreliable narration and intertextuality. Postmodernists often challenge authority and it was visible in their experimental literature. Irony, playfulness, black humor, multiple voices, fragmented narrative structure and intertexuality form the essence of postmodern literary works. Usage of parody and pastiche is deliberately done to represent the fictional nature of work which is nothing but constructed. It embraces fragmentation and disorientation and decentres logocentric approach. Postmodernists believe that there is no centre that holds absolute power. According to Derrida, the centre is constantly moving towards the periphery and the periphery aims moving towards the centre. The centre which represents power is never absolute and the periphery is engaged in gaining that power, in this process the centre is decentred, thus acquiring multiple centres. This postponement of centre is what Derrida calls 'differance'. In literary texts therefore, single meaning cannot be achieved but the text leaves gaps for multiple interpretations. Postmodernist fiction unsettles and deconstructs traditional notions about language, about representations and also about writing. For example, the representation of woman, mother, motherhood is revisited and given new interpretation in postmodern context.

Summing Up

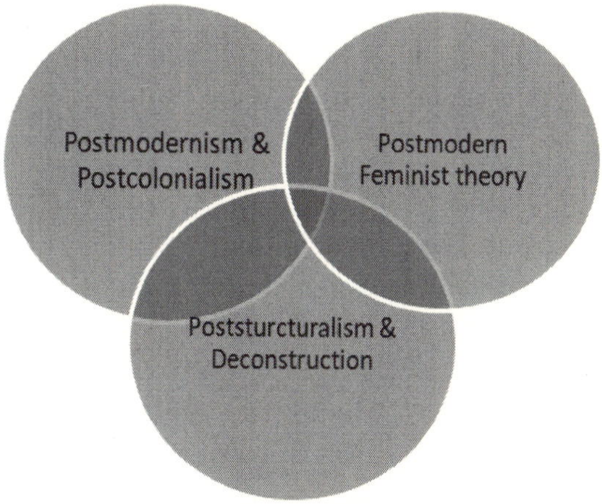

Figure 2 shows intersection of the three schools of thoughts

Some Postmodern tendencies
Text as Unstable and dynamic
Desire for flows, shifts, instability in meaning
Celebration of fragmentation, playfulness
Celebration of multiplicity, heterogeneity and differences
Deconstruction/Subversion of constructed ideas/binaries
Resistance to 'constructs' and hegemonic grand narratives
Intertextuality, hybridity, metafiction, parody, magic realism
Postmodern feminist theory

2.4. Problematising Identity

Postmodernism advocates multiplicity, pluralism, and open endedness. This is much applicable to the concept of identity as well, which is much discussed by postmodern writers. And Kapur is no exception. Kapur's novels portray the plurality of female experiences and how each woman adopts different strategies for self-assertion and constructive growth. This chapter seeks to analyse the issues pertaining to the idea of identity as discussed in Kapur's works. It explores how her texts address different identities thus indicating the multiplicity of the idea of identity. Some of the identities under question are diaspora identity, sexual identity, cultural identity and self-identity. Kapur subverts these ideologies and projects that identities are fractured or fragmented representations.

In postmodern and postcolonial discourses, the issue of identity is a much-debated topic. Many postcolonial theorists have given their opinion that identity is a constructed idea. Judith Butler subverts the idea of fixed identity. Judith Butler claims that gender is performatively created and there is no pre-existing gender identity.

> "There is no gender identity behind the expression of gender; that identity is performatively constituted by the very "expressions" that are said to be its results (34).

Butler's notion of identity subverts the fixed, static state of identity. Social codes dictate that one needs to perform one's gender identity. The compulsory heterosexuality imposed by the patriarchal culture in a heteronormative world limits an individual's sexual preferences. Emergent homosexual, gay, lesbian and queer groups and their movements is a strategy to resist the unitary, monolithic identity created by dominant culture.

Edward Said too joins this debate on identity and his *Orientalism* discusses at length postcolonial theories and touches upon the idea of identity. The identities of the orients are western constructs and representations. In this context, Edward Said's words bear significance. Said too challenges such unitary notion of identity and advocates the dismantling of such totalising concept. For him:

> Identity does not necessarily imply ontologically given and eternally determined stability or uniqueness, or irreducible character, or a privileged status as something total and complete in itself (315).

Homi Bhaba, another postcolonial theorist also suggests that the identities of the coloniser and the colonised are not fixed but rather instable. Bhaba questions the notion of stable identity by exploring how the homogeneous identity imposed upon the colonial subject is resisted. Instead of looking at identity as fixed and complete concept, Bhaba comes with the opinion that the identity of the colonial subject is hybrid. Edward Said too favours this opinion that identities are of fluid nature and not fixed.

Diasporic communities undergo cultural transformation. Therefore, diasporic existence uproots the notion of fixed, rooted identities. Diaspora embraces multiple, hybrid identities.

Cultural theorist Stuart Hall and Michel Foucault offer insights into identity and call upon cultural identity as a constant process of construction and reconstruction. The idea is elaborated though the concept of 'discourse' that problematises the notion of fixed autonomous identity. Stuart Hall offers critical insights into the formation of cultural identity. Like other postmodern theorists, Hall argues that identities are never complete, finished products; rather, they are constantly in the process of construction and reconstruction. Michel Foucault's perception is deconstruction of dominant discourse that imposes monolithic identity to individuals. Foucault problematises this issue of identity by bringing in the idea of 'discourse' and he argues 'discourse' gives rise to the formation of identities. Foucault calls for the deconstruction of dominant discourses that imposes monolithic identities.

Jacques Derrida questions the binary oppositions in western humanist philosophy and goes ahead to decenter and destabilise these hierarchies, one among them is the notion of identity. Jacques Derrida whose deconstructive approaches to western philosophy especially that of binary oppositions like male/female, white/black, coloniser/colonised etc. in which the first occupies a upper hand over the other. Derrida deconstructs this hierarchical opposition and questions what the 'centre' occupies. Postmodernism offers opportunity to celebrate plurality.

This postcolonial discourse on the issue of identity has left vast impact on postcolonial writers like Manju Kapur. Kapur's works do explore the multifarious nature of identity and its formation in the contemporary times. The issue of identity has been an important thematic concern for Indian English writings. Identities are constructive in nature. Kapur's texts explore the multidimensional nature of identity. Kapur problematises the issue of identity. The notion of identity should not be read as water tight compartments but as negotiable, readjustable and fluid.

In diasporic condition, people would have relocated for various reasons, but they maintain cultural ties with their homeland through memories and practices. Because of dislocation and relocation, people encounter cultural transformation. Diaspora, Homi Bhaba argues, contests the notions of fixed, rooted identity. Babha looks at the borders as 'in-between' spaces where identities are re-formed. Diasporic people are in a state of in-betweenness, oscillating between their home country and the country adopted.

Drastic developments in the field of science and technology, trade and commerce, telecommunication technologies have led to what we call as global community where multiculturalism and pluralism are key phenomenology. In this context, selfhood and identity bears a significant thought and analysis especially in the postmodern context. This chapter will explore the various identities as confronted in Kapur's texts and towards the end will point out how these 'identities' that we talk about are itself fragmentary in nature and this is what the author seems to show.

The term identity is a multidimensional word. One may talk of individual identity, national identity, cultural identity, diaspora identity and also sexual identity. We have also heard of writer's identity, identity of Indian English writers and so on. Indian English fiction has been able to capture and explore these identities in a subtle manner. In most of the narratives of postmodern texts, the crisis of identity is well captured. Even before that, Mulk Raj has explored the hidden dimensions of human psyche especially the lower section of people what we today call as Dalits. East-west confrontations and the resulting cultural dilemma explicitly surface in much of R. K. Narayan's fiction. Anita Desai's fiction explores individual psyche especially the mind of women. Her fiction centers around few characters and the narrative follows the stream of consciousness technique. Her fiction explores self-identity and diaspora identity with a feministic touch. The crisis of identity and the efforts to locate it along the finite dimensions of the narrative forms the major bulk of her thematic concern. Salman Rushdie's *Midnight Children (1980) and Shame (1983)* are both knit around the idea of identity crisis and the author attempts to confront the life of individual and that of nation and its history. *The Satanic Verses* published in 1988 explores the religious identity of an Asian expatriate in England. In the literary arena, Amitav Ghosh's *The Shadow Lines* once again explores individual and national identity. Arundhati Roy's *The God of Small Things* resonates the complexity of identity crisis in the chain of human relationships. It is clear from a close survey of Indian English writers and their concerns that identity is the central focus and major platform for their exploration of other issues as well. The advent of newer technologies and the expansion of education, gave shape to the different concepts of identity. Post 1980 is the era of transition and change in belief systems. The growth of multi-national companies and multiculturalism challenged some of the traditional value system. With easier accessibility to transport, communication and employment opportunities, people are willing to explore more. Hence crossing international border for various reasons have become no longer a distant dream for many.

Summing Up

Postcolonial Discourses on identity
Challenges/subverts the idea of fixed identity
Result of action, performance
Identity forms through repetition and imitation
Free, flexible, instable, fluid and continuous process
Exposes limiting nature of identity categories
Subverts ideologies and projects that identities are fractured or fragmented representations
Diasporic communities undergo cultural transformation. Diaspora embraces multiple, hybrid identities
Foregrounds Queer theory

Postcolonial Theorists	
Judith Butler	Gender Identity as 'construct' and unnatural
Edward Said	Identities of the orients are western constructs and representations. Challenges such unitary notion of identity and advocates the dismantling of such totalising concept
Homi K. Bhaba	Questions the notion of stable identity. Homogeneous identity is resisted. States identities are of fluid nature and not fixed. Talks about Hybrid identity
Stuart Hall & Michel Foucault	Cultural identity: identities are never complete, finished products; rather they are constantly in the process of construction and reconstruction
Jacques Derrida	Questions the binary oppositions in western humanitst philosophy, decenters and destabilises these hierarchies, one such is the notion of identity

Manju Kapur has also consistently explored the issue of identity in her novels. Her novels offer interesting ways of understanding the problematics of identity. Kapur explores the multiple ways in which our identities are constructed and offers us critical insight into multidimensionality of identity. Kapur seems to articulate that identity is a matter of conscious choice. Identity is fragmentary resulting in hybrid identities. Identity itself is a signifier, signifying so many identities and thus resulting in an ongoing and never-ending process, open ended rather than fixed and closed entity. In *Difficult Daughters*, Kapur talks about national identity and the identity yearned by women. Identity becomes a heavily constructed discourse. One of the important aspects of identity is that it needs to be continuously negotiated. Nina in *The Immigrant* for example has to negotiate with the markers of Indian identity be it food or dress and consciously adopts to situations based on need. So, the markers of Indian identity are also subject to change especially for the diaspora population. In a diasporic existence, displacement offers newer understanding of the concept of identity. Kapur's fictional works in some or other way problematise the very idea of identity and while doing so, does not arrive at or provide any concrete solution. They are left open ended to suggest that we must assimilate what seems proper and correct to one's mind and not stick to anything blindly. Kapur, like other postmodern writers, deconstructs the idea of identity. She explores national identity, identity of women, sexual identity, cultural identity and the diaspora identity. In fact, the term Indian English writing itself became a much debatable topic questioning the authenticity in portraying Indianess or the Indian identity. Postcolonial discourses treat identity as a continuous process which means it is subject to change.

2.5 Diasporic Identity

People leave their homeland and migrate to different territories for various reasons. Migration to other countries in search of better education, employment opportunities, growth and comfort is a common trend these days. Migrating to different land for various purposes is something very common with the beginning of the 21st century; perhaps largely due to globalisation and the rise in multinational companies. Thus, we have different Diasporas taking its form – for e.g., the African diaspora, the Asian diaspora, the Indian diaspora and so on. The size of Indian diaspora community has been increasing in the post globalisation era especially in the UK and American countries. Education and employment opportunities, life with luxury, freedom and ease is what tempted many to explore these countries. These diaspora communities are not free from certain issues like racial differences, being 'othered', loneliness, loss of cultural values that was found difficult to sustain, cultural assimilation and rootlessness.

The Indian Diaspora is estimated to be the second largest in the world and has a diversified global presence. Emigration of highly skilled professionals, workers and students migrating to developed countries, particularly to the USA, UK, Canada,

Australia and New Zealand is observed. This flow started after Indian independence and gathered momentum with the emigration of IT professionals in the 1990s.

Sudesh Mishra in his essay "From Sugar to Masala" divides the Indian diaspora into two categories – the old and the new. He writes:

> This distinction is between, on the one hand, the semi-voluntary flight of indentured peasants to non-metropolitan plantation colonies such as Fiji, Trinidad, Mauritius, South Africa, Malaysia, Surinam, and Guyana, roughly between the years 1830 and 1917; and the other the late capital or postmodern dispersal of new migrants of all classes to thriving metropolitan centres such as Australia, the United States, Canada, and Britain (276).

Especially after Indian independence, the Indian diasporic community has acquired a new identity due to the processes of self-fashioning and increasing acceptance by the West. Individuals who migrate may appear to be in a comfort zone but there are certain realities that cannot be denied; the loss of cultural norms, religious customs, and social support systems, adjustment to a new culture and changes in identity and concept of self. Indian English fiction captures some of these sentiments of an individual's need of assimilation into a new land, a new world of pluralistic and hybrid culture. Contemporary Indian Diaspora writers like Anita Desai, Salman Rushdie, V. S. Naipaul, Bharathi Mukherjee, Jhumpa Lahiri, Kiran Desai, Vikram Chandra and others have explored themes of alienation, existential rootlessness, nostalgia, protest and assertions, quest of identity, autonomy, cultural clash, and confrontations with racism and so on. The novels of the older generation of diasporic Indian writers like Raja Rao, G. V. Desani, Santha Rama Rau, Balachandra Rajan, Nirad Chaudhuri, and Ved Mehta predominantly look back at India and record their experiences away from India as expatriates. They look at their homeland from a distance and this gives in their writing an objectified perspective. The distance affords them the detachment that is so necessary to have a clear perception of their native land. In that sense, through their writing, they help to define India. The modern diasporic Indian writers can be grouped into two distinct classes. One class comprises those who have spent a part of their life in India and have carried the baggage of their native land offshore. They are the first generation of immigrants for whom migration creates alienation, nostalgia of the past, and a sense of rootlessness. This sense of displacement and dislocation creates a position of living 'in-between' where there is this sense of one's own bonding to cultural roots and the other a resistance to accept the codes of the new land. This gives birth to double consciousness. The other class comprises the second generation, children born of immigrants are those who have been bred since childhood outside India. They have a view of their country only from the outside as an exotic place of their origin. The country of their birth is not similar to the country of their origin. The writers of the former group have a literal displacement whereas those belonging to the latter group find themselves rootless. The second generation of immigrants too faces alienation, their identity shaped by the country of the birth and the other held strongly by their parents. Consciousness of both the identities and a sense of 'in-betweenness' result in identity crisis or hybrid identity. Hence, most of the new generation of immigrants evolve themselves by adopting the elements of both cultures and attempt to assimilate to form a hybrid identity. Both the groups of writers have produced an enviable corpus of English literature. These writers while depicting migrant characters in their fiction explore the theme of displacement and self-fashioning. The diasporic Indian writers' depiction of dislocated characters gains immense importance if seen against the geo-political background of the vast Indian subcontinent. That is precisely why such works have a global readership and an enduring appeal. The diasporic Indian writers have generally dealt with characters from their own displaced community but some of them have also taken a liking for Western characters and they have been convincing in dealing with them. Two of the earliest novels that have successfully depicted diasporic Indian characters are Anita Desai's *Bye-Bye Blackbird* and Kamala Markandaya's *The Nowhere Man*. These novels depict how racial prejudice against Indians in the UK of the 1960s alienates the characters and aggravate their sense of displacement. Bharati Mukherjee's novels like *Wife* and *Jasmine* depict Indians in the US – the land of immigrants, both legal and illegal – before globalisation got its impetus. Salman Rushdie in the novel *The Satanic Verses* approaches the allegory of migration by adopting the technique of magic realism. Chitra Banerjee Divakaruni in her novel *The Mistress of Spices* depicts Tilo, the protagonist, as an exotic character to bring out the migrant's angst. Amitav Ghosh's novel *The Shadow Lines* has the character Ila whose father is a roaming diplomat and whose upbringing has been totally on foreign soils. She finds herself as much out of place in India as any foreigner. But when she conjures up the story of her doppelganger Magda being rescued by Nick Price from Denise, it shows the extent of her sense of rootlessness. Amit Chaudhuri in his novel *Afternoon Raag* portrays the lives of Indian students in Oxford. Similarly, Anita Desai in the second part of her novel *Fasting, Feasting* depicts Arun as a migrant student living in the suburbs of Massachusetts. Thus, various diasporic Indian writers have skillfully brought out the various issues hidden within the corpus of diaspora sensibility.

Manju Kapur is unlike other diaspora writers. She has gone abroad for studies but not for a settlement. She lives in India and explores the lives of Indians as she sees them around. Interestingly, it is only in her novel, *The Immigrant*, she brings to surface the various forces that make Indians to migrate, the consequences, and the gradual acceptance and the willingness to adapt and adopt for convenience in a globalised world. As the story unfolds, we see that Kapur, looks into the aspect of migration in a very very practical way. The reality presented is that these days' migration cannot be related to exile because that kind of life is consciously chosen, either for better prospects or personal commitments. Hence, the sense of alienation, cultural conflict, and isolation is already anticipated and painfully undertaken and more often the character is seen as assimilating a hybrid culture and identity. In this discourse, Kapur, questions and deconstructs the very notion of identity; as there is nothing as 'one concrete identity' and that the identity that we speak about is subject to change. Kapur's characters, especially the women protagonists realise selfhood as freedom, choice, rights, equality, rationality and control of one's self. Her protagonists are poised between submission and resistance, passivity and action. The very instability of this subject contains, within it, the possibility of initiating a change.

Kapur's *The Immigrant* has very minimal characters unlike her other novels. The central character is Nina and the story unfolds with a description of her as a thirty-year-old single woman whose mother is obsessed with a need to find a suitable groom for her. Nina is educated, good looking and works as college lecturer. The story engages us with Nina's life, her marriage with Ananda, a NRI settled in Canada as a dentist. Nina goes to Canada after marriage as an immigrant and her journey of life in a new environment begins. In Kapur's *The Immigrant*, marriage becomes the reason for relocation to a foreign land. For Nina, it is marriage; whereas for her husband, it is education and job that keeps his stay there. Nina is presented before us as dutiful Indian girl, a lecturer in a prestigious college and her mother is curious about her daughter's marriage. In the initial pages of the book, Nina represents Indian womanhood and her Indianess mark her national identity. She crosses oceans to get settled with her new life, and after facing initial phases of loneliness and homesickness, learns to adopt and adapt to the environment and culture. But as the novel progresses, we see that her Indian identity gives way to American way of life. This transition happens incidentally primarily because of her husband's indifference to their marital life. Kapur takes the individual problem of the family, in this case Ananda's incompatibility in sexual relation with his wife and the related problems. Nina and Ananda do represent diaspora community and the transition to American ways is individual choice for Ananda but a catharsis for Nina whose marital discord has left her to find more meanings while adapting to a new system of life. Kapur, perhaps, hints to say that diaspora existence is individual choice and freedom and identity is subject to change.

Nina suffers from double displacement. After marriage, she had to shed her economically self-sufficient status of being a professor and move on to a foreign land where both the land and her husband are new to her. She had to get along with family, her marital life and also the newly acquainted culture and environment. Initially, Nina suffers from alienation, but gradually knows to adapt to situation. The clash between one's native culture and of the accepted land gives rise to the dilemma of which one to accept or ignore. This gives rise to the idea of double identity which gives way to one's perception of the world through the consciousness of colonisers as well through one's vision, provided and taught by native culture. The concept of identity and rootedness is questioned. One's clothing, physical appearance, colour of the skin, name, native language, accent and pronunciation, mannerism and the food taken speak volumes about one's identity even though distantly located. The dilemma of acceptance or rejection of norms runs through the immigrant's life in the new culture. His identity swings between two cultures and it remains as double identity.

Kapur talks about the immigrant psyche:

> These immigrants are always in two minds. Outwardly they adjust well. Educated and English speaking, they allow misleading assumptions about a heart that is divided. In the new country, they work lengthy hours to gain entrance into the system, into society, into establishing a healthy bank account (The Immigrant 123).

Nina confronts racial discrimination at the airport in Canada although having a valid passport and Visa.

> The immigration woman examines each page of her passport suspiciously. Nina's claim that she has married a citizen needs to be scrutinised despite the paperwork. The colour of her skin shouts volumes in that small room. She feels edgy; she is alone with a woman who makes no eye contact, for whom she is less than human (The Immigrant 106).

The sense of displacement and the flux between two cultures – of the coloniser and the colonised is experienced by Nina in Canada. "For the first time in her life she felt out of place. Wrong clothes, shoes, handbag, bag. May be in their eyes she was like the women sweeping" (*The Immigrant* 104).

Nina and Ananda and his uncle represent the Indian diasporic community. Kapur's concerns are the Indian emigrants who face different challenges in adjusting to a new environment. Kapur shows the complexity in life of a newly wed Indian woman through the protagonist Nina. Issues of identity, of rootlessness, confrontations with racism, nostalgia for the homeland, cultural in-betweenness, double identity, of being 'othered' and the theme of individuality are the aspects dealt with as the story moves ahead with different episodes. Kapur skillfully shows us the intricacies and problems of human psyche, especially the phenomenology of Indian women.

One striking observation is how Kapur talks about the way women are subjected to patriarchy and tradition and the same is resonated through mothers in the novel who want their daughters to get married, bear children, look after family and follow traditions. In the contrary, fathers are shown having better regard for their daughters. They support daughters in acquiring higher education and being independent. Father figures seem to be much more understanding. Nisha's father, Astha's father and Virmati's father are all supportive of their daughters having education, career and being independent.

Apart from narrating the immigrant lives of the couple, the novelist has fused the Indian political scenario of 1975 to 1977 in this fiction as a background.

There is this kind of resistance and acceptance of ideology. Kapur also indicates skin colour as an immigrant issue. The white colour takes superior position when juxtaposed with black or brown skin. Nina felt ashamed about her skin colour although in India it was considered as a prized fair complexion.

> I am the wrong colour; I came from the wrong place...... of all the passengers the only one not allowed to sail through

immigration, made to feel like an illegal alien (*The Immigrant* 107).

A sense of loss is prominent in the novels which deal with the issues of immigrants. Nostalgia, a sense of loneliness, compromise and adjustment is what every immigrant confronts. Nina's feelings are similar to that of Ashima in Jhumpa Lahiri's *The Namesake*. Ashima realises that "being a foreigner is a sort of lifelong pregnancy – a perpetual wait, a constant burden…." (33).

Nina experiences absolute freedom, freedom from the probing eyes of family members, neighbours, domestic help and so on. She was all for herself. This freedom and marital breakdown lead to an extramarital relationship, vegetarianism to eating flesh and shedding aside norms and taboos. She wanted adventure and experience the 'road not taken'. She felt that there was no going back but to head fresh territories. She asserts 'when one is reinventing oneself, anywhere could be home' (330).

Thus, Manju Kapur shows how transmigrants moving across different cultures and locations are caught physically and psychologically between two worlds. The displacement that we talk of is not only geographical, and cultural but also spiritual. The love for privacy and independence as advocated by westerners are gradually imbibed by the immigrants. The theme of displacement and cultural identity is predominant here. The themes and areas of discussion as projected by Manju Kapur is also experimented by other diasporic writers of Indian origin who more or less address similar kind of issues.

2.6 Cultural Identity

When we say culture, immediately we ask what it signifies. Any culture represents or signifies itself through verbal and non-verbal forms. Language, clothing, food, behavior, mannerism, belief system, ideologies, names, colour of the skin, celebrations and rituals, upbringing all are markers of a particular culture. When a child is born, it gradually imbibes with it the cultural practices of its society. Kapur's fiction are clearly Indian fiction as they represent the Indian identity. Kapur's texts have Indian names, ample usage of food imagery, the settings and locale, the Indianised usage of the English language, idioms and phrases common in India are all elaborately used. So, at once it becomes a text where an Indian reader can attach himself to. For a non-Indian reader, the text itself becomes a cultural signifier as literature is byproduct of a particular culture. But this cultural identity which we associate ourselves to is also subject to fragmentation or change. Kapur's texts question the authentication of these cultural markers. In *The Immigrant,* Ananda, an Indian name becomes Andy in Canada and Ananda enjoys being called by this Americanised name. His wife Nina finds awkward when people stare at her clothes (sarees) and the bangles she wears at the airport in Toronto. She had to shed these clothes and choose western clothes so as to suit the weather and to feel at home in a new land. Food, too, takes a new turn. The initial pages of the text were filled with descriptions of Indian foods like dal, sabji, parathas and so on but as transition occurs description of foods like cheese, butter, beef seem to frequent.

Folk narratives, myths and the stories depicted in the epics and puranas also constitute to its cultural metaphor. These narratives tell how man or woman is expected to behave or have behaved. Goddesses like Parvati, Sita or Kannaki are seen as upholder of virtue and societal norms. They embody archetypal images which represent dutifulness, obedience and feminine qualities; whereas Goddess Kali becomes a symbol of power and revolt.

Clothes reveal our identity, habit and personality. Detachment to traditional clothes and welcoming western wear gives modern women status. But woman who move abroad change to clothing styles, either out of compulsion or the sheer necessity of the environment. So, an immigrant like Nina would need to shed her comfortable clothes and get into something which feels 'like being more exposed'. There is this transition, change and acceptance.

> As immigrants fly across oceans they shed their
> Old clothing, because clothes make the man
> And new ones help ease the transition (*The Immigrant* 150).

Name is a part of human identity and it reflects the culture, tradition, religion, region, race and gender of any person. A name of a person speaks so many things, it is filled with meanings. A name of a person is also related to some God or some myths. In *The Immigrant*, Ananda wants him to be called as Andy which Nina dislikes. Perhaps, Ananda gets a psychological relief when he chooses himself to be called in a westernised name.

Cultural signifier is emphasised in the description of the Indian restaurant which Ananda and Nina visit to have an Indian meal. Kapur explains: "A pleated sari hung on the wall, a miniature Taj Mahal glowed in the red lights under a glass case on the counter...." (141) But the couple found the taste only close to authenticity. The restaurant itself symbolises cultural hybridity in an alien land. The food which is only close to the orginal taste becomes a metaphor for hybridity.

Food becomes a cultural identity and a marker. Ananda and Nina in *The Immigrant* leave aside their vegetarian habits and switch to meat eating. Indian practices were left aside by justifying it to adapting to a new land. Each break was substantiated with reasonable arguments: "How long could one hang on to caste taboos, for whom and for what? (32) How did one's identity depend on what he ate?" (35)

Name, habit, food, clothing, practices are all cultural markers and in *The Immigrant*, they are markers of Indian identity and these markers undergo a change in a foreign land. Kapur deconstructs the idea of unitary concept of identity itself and identity is itself shaped by our social surroundings. The idea of hybrid identity gets reinforced. The tension in the narrative between Indianness and global hybridity is reflected in the texture of the writing. Kapur's trade mark of culinary lexical comes before: "She soaked dals and imli, she ground the walnuts for her special burfi, she fried namak para" (52). This list is paralleled by North American consumer goods. "corn chips, salt and vinegar chips, onion and garlic dip. Mint and coconut chocolate. Cinnamon sweets. Buttery shortbread biscuits" (180).

As Nina identifies with the North American counterpart, the Indian culinary lexical becomes thinner. Food also governs one's identity.

> That Monday Nina walked to the library, fish and beef indelibly part of her being. Feeling less Indian had its advantages. There were more possibilities in the world she could be open to. Her body was her own – and that included her digestive system and her vagina (268).

In Indian society, maternity becomes an occasion for celebration as motherhood is given prime importance. After marriage, every woman is expected to bear children. The society and its culture associate the status of a woman to being a married woman and becoming a mother. The attainment of puberty is celebrated in societies which is a way of declaring the girl's fertility. Even some rituals accompanied in a marriage are seen as a positive gateway for the attainment of motherhood. Indian culture glorifies motherhood and when this is not attained by a woman, her life is lost. Infertility is viewed as deviance from the cultural norm, rendering woman helpless and also becoming the ground for divorce. In *Custody*, Kapur seems to negotiate with a different kind of mothering in an expecting culture. Ishita is childless, lost love from her in-laws and ultimately her marriage ended in divorce. Later, she becomes the step mother for Raman's daughter. Kapur negotiates the stigma of infertility and reconstructs a different reality in which motherhood is attained through alternative ways – by adoption. French critic Simone de Beauvoir has argued that from infancy women are told about their role of childbearing. Such pervasive socialisation makes women to desire for motherhood. Against this, Ishita emerges as a 'New Woman' who embraces a different way of being a mother and regaining a status. The issue of infertility and motherhood is a recurrent concern in Kapur's fiction.

Sagun in *Custody* embraces a different life altogether. She represents a class where women desire subjects not objects with a longing for sexual expression, satisfaction and fulfillment. For Shagun, body becomes the scope for a different world: a world of love, expression and happiness. Ishita, on the other hand, condemns her body as her fallopian tubes are blocked and cannot produce children. For her, body becomes a site for social stigma, depression, torture and psychological pressure. Her husband's house punishes her for substandard body. Kapur has drawn our attention to this cultural and social identity of a woman where her identity is shaped in terms of marriage and maternity.

2.7 Self-identity

When we talk about self-identity, it is about the individual consciousness. The idea of self-realisation, being assertive and to value oneself forms self-identity. Kapur's fiction largely deal with the exploration of a woman's identity; how a woman's identity is shaped in a society and what the woman wants to be considered as her own identity. Each of her novels begins with a conventional set up. Families wanting their young girls to be married, women who are driven towards the conventional way of life and so on set the beginning of the novels. But as the novels proceed, we find the women characters becoming self-aware, bold, assertive and give vent to their opinions and ideas. They realise that they need some space for themselves, make their own lives and understand the need for autonomy. Self-identity is something that they look for. Kapur's protagonists realise their marginal positions and comprehend the way in which they have been "othered". They re-define identity and chalk out strategies of resistance. Kapur's women not only set in the idea of 'New Woman' but also reject the fixed categories of identity and look for expressions of self through multiple forms. What we today presume as our identity undergoes change. In *Difficult Daughters*, Virmati at first wants to be recognised as Harish's wife. She wants the professor to give her the status of his wife. During that time her concern was to gain wifely status and to become complete in that sense. Virmati's idea of identity, at that point of time, is to gain her identity in the society as his wife. But after getting that status, she is not happy because she has to overcome other problems that creep within the family. All she does is 'adjust, compromise and adapt'. Nina in her immigrant experience struggles for selfhood in a newly adopted land. She rejects old customs, beliefs, style, sacrifices her habits and perception to fit into the existing system.

In *Home*, Sona and Rupa, two contrasting sisters have different ambitions. For Sona, bearing children and having a 'complete' family is her preoccupation; whereas Rupa who, like her sister, is unable to conceive takes an alternate focus and diverts herself to pickle business. Similarly, in *Custody,* there are two contrasting women. Ishita who is childless, is happy to be married to Raman and to mother his daughter; whereas Shagun wants freedom, flexibility and happiness. For Shagun, her sexuality brings her power, freedom and autonomy.

In *A Married Woman*, Astha cries out "I need more space" (156). In the initial pages of the fiction, Astha's upbringing, her heterosexual fantasies go on 'normal' lines, but towards the end there is a swift in sexual preferences. Sexual identity is not fixed. Normalcy gets subverted.

Nostalgia fills Nina in *The Immigrant.* After coming to Canada, she listens to Kumbh mela and is nostalgic about her country... the novelist says:

> Even though she despised cheap nostalgia, the way she reacted to the Kumbh Mela was proof that living in a different country you became a different person (177).

The Immigrant ends with a positive note from Nina:

> Perhaps that was the ultimate immigrant experience. Not that any one thing was steady enough to attach yourself to for the rest of your life, but that you found different ways to belong, ways not necessarily lasting, but ones that made your journey less lonely for a while. When something failed it was a signal to move on. For an immigrant, there was no going back. – When one was reinventing oneself, anywhere could be home. Pull up your shallow roots and move. Find a new place, new friends, a new family. It had been possible once, it would be possible again (334).

Shagun is a bold character portrayed in *Custody.* Against all odd ends, she wants to regain her identity, individuality and freedom. To achieve this, she goes all miles and at the cost of losing her daughter to Raman.

Kapur's women Virmati, Astha, Nisha, Nina, Shagun and Ishita all strive for self-identity. In this struggle for individuality, they are caught between values, traditions, ethics and societal pressures, yet they are bold enough to resist and emerge strongly to fight in order to achieve freedom of expression and thought.

2.8 Sexual Identity

Marriage as an institution administered in heterosexual society controls women's free will. Many women writers have pointed that in the given patriarchal set up, women not only are managed and controlled but are expected to keep the tradition rolling by passing it to their daughters. The tussle between tradition and modernity and mother-daughter relation within this nexus becomes an oft explored subject. Rigid codes of 'appropriate' behaviour and internalisation of these gendered codes governs women's psyche and compels them to bear the torch of tradition, rituals and beliefs which are often restrictive and oppressive.

Historically, women's minds are conditioned to act out, following Judith Butler's idea of 'gendered performances.' In *Bodies that Matter*, Butler talks about the construction, repetition and reproduction of the sexual subject which according to her is a temporal process, which operates through the reiteration of norms and the sexual subject is both produced and destabilised in the course of this reiteration. She argues,

> Construction is neither a single act nor a causal process initiated by a subject and in a set of fixed effects...As a sedimented effect of a reiterative or ritual practice, sex acquires its naturalised effect, and, yet, it is also by virtue of this reiteration that gaps and fissures are opened up as the constitutive instabilities in such constructions, as that which escapes or exceeds the norm, as that which cannot be wholly defined or fixed by the repetitive labor of that norm (Butler 10).

In her notable work, *Gender Trouble*, Butler argues that gender operates everywhere and is set of 'performances'. All actions that are considered appropriate for men and women have been transmitted and repeated to produce a situation or environment that both maintains and legitimises a seemingly natural gender binary. According to her, heteronormative bodies and sexualities are constructed phenomenon to hold the power discourses. Butler's theories interface gender and queer studies; especially the ideas associated with stigmatisation. Any deviation from the constructed 'normal' goes for stigmatisation and unacceptance. Butler contests that the multitude ways that people are shamed or positioned as 'different' should not be understood as a consequence of their being or actions; rather, the root cause of all this is when something is conceived as 'normal'. The process of 'gendering' paves women's bodies to be considered beyond normalcy or deviant and anything deviant is othered in heterosexual context.

In *Undoing Gender* (2004), Butler discusses how 'performativity' is 'automatic or mechanical' and argues that desires do not emerge from personhood but from social norms. Butler distinguishes 'Performance' from 'Performativity' saying that 'Performativity' means an act that not only communicates but also creates an identity. This becomes source of construction of gender categories and identities. Butler's ideas greatly influenced and mobilised understanding of gender, sexuality and queer representations.

With these discourses, queer theory developed, challenging the 'socially constructed' categories of sexual categorisation and identity. Queer theory deploys the tenets put forward by post-structuralists and like the concept of fragmented identities, hold sexuality as fluid and dynamic. It defies the heterosexuality as standard norm and explores the idea of multiple sexualities like bisexuality, homosexuality or lesbianism. Any fixity in sexual orientation is called into question. Queer theory, thus, questions the traditional binary constructions of sexuality. The heteronormativity which makes heterosexuality the privileged social norm is contested through the discourse of queer sexualities.

Adrienne Cecile Rich, an American poet, essayist and feminist is notable for her famous 1980 essay on "Compulsory Heterosexuality and Lesbian Existence". Adrienne Rich argues that heterosexuality is not "natural" or intrinsic in human instincts, but an institution imposed upon by many cultures and societies which transits women to a subordinate situation. In this very essay, she used the term 'compulsory heterosexuality' to represent how institutions like family and marriage proliferate heterosexuality as legitimate and standard. Heterosexuality, thus, becomes the dominant discourse than 'others' deviant forms of sexualities such as lesbianism which is considered a threat to dominant form. Lesbianism demonstrates a contrary to the established norms and beliefs set by heterosexual family system.

She argues that heterosexuality itself is a powerful political institution that subordinates women and permits "male right of physical, economical, and emotional access" to women. According to her, women can explore other forms of sexuality like lesbianism and practice with their free will. It was not written to widen divisions but to encourage heterosexual feminists to examine heterosexuality as a political institution which disempowers women. Rich sees lesbian existence as an act of resistance to this institution, but also as an individual choice. Lesbian identity throws heterosexuality into question and challenges it. She argues that it is a kind of resistance to compulsory heterosexuality to a cultural system that forces women to desire for men. That woman should have their own sexual preferences and shall not have anything forced unto them. Rich claims that women may not have a preference toward heterosexuality, but may find it imposed, managed, organised, propagandised, and maintained by society. She observes:

> The assumption that 'most women are innately heterosexuals' stands as a theoretical and political stumbling block for many women. It remains a tenable assumption, partly because lesbian existence has been written out of history or catalogued under disease; partly because it has been treated as exceptional rather than intrinsic; partly because to acknowledge that for women

> heterosexuality may not be a 'preference' at all but something that has had to be imposed, managed, organised, propagandised and maintained by force is an immense step to take if you consider yourself freely and 'innately' heterosexual.... (Rich 119)

One can clearly see that postmodern writers were open in approach and brought to the forefront things which were considered a taboo in the Indian society. Sexual frankness and making a bold attempt to reveal realities characterise a postmodern writer. One such area that remained unexplored earlier was the same sex relationships. Although a sensitive and a taboo in Indian society, contemporary writers have chosen to write on homosexual themes. Ismat Chugtai's short story *Lihaaf* (*The Quilt*) (1941) written during the pre-independence era did not have many followers. Homosexuality was not openly discussed because of societal pressures and patriarchal construction and was considered against social codes set for men and women. Kamala Das's autobiography *My Story* reflects a bold expression of desire and passion for a friend at the boarding school and the author's attraction to other women in her life. Kamala Das wrote in a period where same sex love was considered a public shame. Another autobiographical work that dealt with lesbianism is *Goja: An Autobiographical Myth* (2000) written by Suniti Namjoshi, a lesbian feminist. In Anita Nair's *Ladies Coupe*, the character Marikolandu learns lesbian love from two foreign mistresses and she tries to experiment on the lessons learnt. Raja Rao, writer, poet and teacher of literature is one of the leading gay rights activists. Raja Rao's *Hostel Room131* (2010) is a novel tracing the budding love story in the hostel of an engineering college. Also, his novel, *The Boyfriend* (2003) is considered the first gay novel written in English in India. Ghalib Shiraz Dhalla's novel '*The Exiles*', is all about a homosexual man's extra-marital relationship. There is a change seen in terms of acceptance and publication of queer fiction. Newer writers are thus experimenting not just the form, but also take thematic issues that were untouched in the literary world. While queer fiction in English language flourishes, there is relatively lesser works touching these issues in regional languages. Deepa Mehta's *Fire* (1996) and Karan Razdan's

Girlfriend in popular Indian cinema which dealt with lesbian desire were subject to criticism and provoked mixed responses. Lesbian desire throws men to the periphery and therefore considered a threat.

Homosexuality in Indian society is not something new. It was prevalent in the society ages before but because it was considered weird relationship it did not come to the open platform. Our ancient texts and sculptures are a testimony to this fact that this idea is not something 'western' or new ideas penetrating the Indian soil. Same sex love in ancient India starts with friendship and leads to intimate relationship. In the ancient epic, *The Mahabharat*a, Krishna and Arjuna share intimate friendship. Ruth Vanita and Kidwai in *Same sex love in India: Readings from Literature and History* (2000) deconstruct the myth that homosexuality is a western import and have discussed many other same sex love in the epic, particularly that of Krishna and Arjuna. While normative heterosexuality and marriage still remain the cultural norm, such transgression was also prevalent in the ancient times. The writers also argue that such relations could be traced in the gods and deity's union. Vatyasana's *Kamasutra* a literary text on sex for pleasure also has received universal recognition. Our ancient texts, paintings and sculptures from different cultures testimony that same sex love was prevalent. Temple sculptures from Konarak and Khajuraho to the Kamasutra and other ancient texts contain enough references to suggest that ancient India accommodated a whole range of sexual behaviours. As justified by Ruth Vanita and Kidwai, it is understood that homosexuality is not something that swept to India from the western impact.

Although other arts had touched this aspect, literary texts remained silent until recently. July 2, 2009 is a milestone in the history of queer activism in India. A historic decision of the Delhi High court which threw away the age-old law set by Lord Macaulay in his famous 'minutes' and thus it overturned the colonial law that had defined same-sex relationships and activity as an "unnatural offence". It was with this Delhi high court's favourable judgment on homosexuality, new era begun and new literatures sprung. In this decision, an aspect of the infamous section 377 of the Indian Penal code by the British in 1860 was nullified on the grounds that the criminalisation of consensual sexual acts in private, infringed the fundamental rights granted to the individual under the Constitution of India. However, the amendment did not say anything and remained silent over woman's desire for another women and lesbianism. But the change in the law brought a new dimension in the literary and the film industry. Films and novels on this subject came out to the public front. Although the reaction was a mixed feeling, there came a new beginning. Women writers like Shobha De, Anita Nair, Manju Kapur have brilliantly touched upon these issues. Shobha De's, *Strange Obsession* (1992), Manju Kapur's *A Married Woman* (2002) and Rita Garg's, *Precursor of Love (*2006) deal with lesbianism. Although, the theme remains the same, the approach and treatment varies in each of these texts. For example, in *Strange Obsession*, the relation between Minx and Amrita is different from Astha-Peelika relation in *A Married Woman.* In the former, Amrita is forced into the relationship because of Minx constant and peculiar obsession, and Amrita wants to escape from that relationship. In *A Married Woman,* both the women fall for one another and they seek solace, emotional support and love in that relationship. Physical intimacy is shown in the novel which is an acceptance from both the parties unlike in *Strange Obsession.* Rita Garg's, *Precursor of Love* is the story of the relation between Amilya and the Girl who is not named. But theirs is shown as a natural attraction for one another and there is no compulsion but they seem to be dependent on one another to fulfill their needs. Indian Playwrights like Vijay Tendulkar and Mahesh Dattani have also explored on gender roles.

A Married woman is a story set in an India of the late 1980s and early 1990s and explores two controversial subjects: Hindu-Muslim confrontation and same sex intimacy. These two controversial issues are neatly interwoven leaving space for varied interpretation. Like in *Difficult Daughters*, the partition history of India becomes a back drop and here it is the sensitive Ram janma-Babri masjid issue. The story revolves around the central character Astha who under parental pressure opts for an arranged marriage with Hemant, a foreign returned business man. Desire and passion are two things which the novel constantly seems to address. Before marriage, Astha develops a crush for Bunty, during her school days. Later in college, she is drawn towards Roshan and also has a physical relation but both of these encounters fail to blossom and finally Astha agrees to marry Hemant. Although, Astha has everything a woman yearns for – a dutiful husband, two children and a comfortable life, yet she finds something hollow within the family structure. She finds Hemant too busy with his work and she feels alienated within her home. To shed away her loneliness, she starts to work as school teacher. She gives vent to her despair and anguish, composing poems and making some sketches. She yearns for Hemanth's love and attention and lack of this brings in a sense of isolation and despair. Her life brings in a turning point when she meets Aijaz Ahmed, a history teacher and the founder of The Street Theatre Group. Astha gets involved with this group and her life sparkles with new found ideas. Aijaz motivates and awakens Astha's social spirit and socialises her thinking. Astha writes a script on the burning issue of Babri Masjid and Ram Janamabhoomi to be dramatised in school. Her intelligence and talent is very much appreciated by Aijaz but all her efforts and achievements gain no attention from Hemant. There develops a tender relationship between Astha and Aijaz. Later, Aijaz and his group is burnt alive for staging such controversial subjects. Inspired by Aijaz's works and ideas, Astha emerges as a social activist and starts taking part in rallies for justice, in spite of much resistance from her family. In this phase of her time, she meets Pipeelika, Aijaz's widowed Hindu wife at Ayodhya where she had come to attend a rally to fight against communal disparity. The initial friendship between the two gradually leads to a lesbian relation which both the women seem to enjoy.

It can be clearly seen that Astha desires for heterosexual relations until she meets Pipeelika. As the heterosexual relations did not blossom, her desire for love and being loved is manifested in the form of same sex relationship. She emerges out to be a homosexual because of her circumstances. She finds solace, comfort and love in the arms of Pipeelika. The passion and longing which she had in her heterosexual desire for Bunty, Rohan, Hemant and Aijaz metamorphoses into a lesbian relation with Pipeelika. Lesbianism can be considered as a protest against patriarchy. Literature and art have been another mode of resistance. Astha fulfills her needs through this newly developed relationship but it can also be viewed as a revolt against patriarchy which she faces in the hands of her husband. Astha craves for her own identity and a life which is more fulfilling. Like other Kapur's protagonists, Astha strives to create a self-identity and independence which makes life more meaningful rather than doing the domestic cores and being only a daughter, wife and mother. Astha yearns for a space for herself. She fights not only for a physical space to work her sketches but also a space which gives individual freedom and expression. Astha says: "There are hollows in my life, and I wanted them filled." (*A Married Woman* 2002) Such an assertion is validated in Elaine Showalter's *A literature of their Own.* Showalter states that the main theme of women literature since 1920 is the quest of 'self-discovery' and 'search for identity' (11-14). On the other hand, Betty Friedan in *The Feminine Mystique* admits that the problem of women is not only of sex but it's about identity crisis. She claims:

> For woman, as for man, the need for self-fulfillment – autonomy, self-realisation, independence, individuality, self-actualisation is as important as the sexual need, with a serious consequence when it is thwarted (448).

Astha emerges as a social activist who fights against societal injustices, oppression and suppression in a patriarchal society. The relation between Pipeelika and Astha signifies a threat to Hemant and his male superiority. Heteronormativity is dismantled and lesbianism emerges to challenge male chauvinism. The title *A Married Woman* indicates the lives of two married women – Astha and Pipeelika. The author through Astha voices the need for rationality in thought and approaches to have a balanced environment where one could tolerate the other. The parallel plots suggest an urge for secularism in thought and practices. Against the backdrop of communal violence and unrest, she shows the conjugal life of Muslim Aijaz and Hindu Pipeelika. Kapur also boldly initiates the trangressive relationship in Ayodhya, in the wake of an anti-communalist rally, and by deliberately making one of the pair the Hindu widow of a secularist Muslim. Kapur's *A Married Woman* truely defines postmodern sensibilities that lend wings to question established norms and give space for bold attempts.

In *A Married Woman*, although Astha transits from heterosexual to homosexual relationship, the latter is only temporal. Both the women are emotionally attached to one another but cannot commit to this relation for long. There is a conflict between desire and duty. This conflict between one's responsibilities as a married woman and one's personal needs leads Astha to part away from Pipeelika. Although both women enjoy physical intimacy and have passion for one another, Kapur has her own way of making them depart. Astha realises her duty towards her family and goes back to the family system and Pipeelika heads to the US for a Ph.D. The author is clear about the tension that arises in the minds of Indian women who because of their sense of tradition and rootedness compromise with their individual self. Astha symbolises many married women who are caught between desire for love and freedom and their obligations towards family life. Thus, Astha tells Pipee:

> I love you, you know how much you Meant to me, I try and prove it every moment we have together, but I can't abandon my family, I can't. May be I should not have looked for my happiness, but I can't help myself. I suppose you think I should not be in a relationship, but I had not foreseen....... I'm sorry I am not like you (*A Married Woman* 242).

In her writings, Kapur has clearly shown her woman protagonist as a victim of biology, gender, domestic violence and patriarchal power structures that set irrational codes on women. The image of ideal womanhood and submissive married status is subverted and the heterosexual relation that marriage legalises is challenged by violating the social codes. Although Astha's incidental lesbian world ends with her decision to stay with heterosexual marriage, family and children, an attempt to defy patriarchy and fight against injustices by emerging as a social activist needs appreciation. Postmodern writers represent their woman protagonist as someone who is not a silent sufferer but as bold, assertive and self-conscious one. Marriage is a signifier for heteronormative conjugal life but this signifier is itself ruptured in *A Married Woman*. Kapur's protagonist challenge and fight against traditional practices; but in some point of their time they succumb to the social codes. Resistance to patriarchal power structures is displayed but at the same time Kapur seems to suggest that Indian women cannot resist their obligation towards family and society.

Astha's bisexual behaviour can be traced as: premarital heterosexual affair with Rohan → marital heterosexual life with Hemant → extra marital heterosexual yearning for Aijaz→ post marital lesbian relationship with Pipeelika and then back to heteronormative conjugal life with Hemant.

Sexual identity is not fixed through gender but the choices one makes. Therefore, there is no fixity in sexuality as it is subject to change as well. Nothing is constant and Astha's different encounters represent the idea generated by deconstructionism that there is nothing fixed and every signifier signifies something else. The fixity of gendered and sexual categories is challenged. What we call sexual identity is ruptured and, in this case, the term 'a married woman' signifies some other signifiers. Here, a married woman is not just associated with husband and family but also the outer world where she participates as a social activist and goes beyond boundaries to fulfill her suppressed desires. *A Married Woman*, as a text subverts the literary tradition of considering these subjects from a negative aspect. In this sense, the text becomes a postcolonial text that attempts to resist the cultural hegemony of colonial/nationalist discourse. The ideal of "womanhood" in this case of a married woman as conceived in the patriarchal society is subverted. The text is a bold attempt to give space and voice to these minorities in the public domain. Although Kapur does not advocate or moralise anything, there is a clear indication of emergence of lesbian identity. Astha's and Pipeelika's relationship does not evolve only in the private spaces. The two in order to be together, visit theaters, restaurants and take journeys together. Again, this is an intentional strategy to represent queer space from the private to the public domain. As the nation witnesses various trials and tribulations in the form of communal disturbances, so is Astha's life filled with disillusionments. There is a desire to stay connected with the relationship that Astha has but this relationship is ruptured and falls apart towards the end of the novel. Astha's family obligation and realisation that her family needs her, makes her difficult to commit to that relation and she accepts her earlier heterosexual family life. In most of Kapur's novels, the woman characters evolve, self-realise their need to be independent, fight against injustices and resist patriarchal norms and codes but at the same time these characters realise that certain things cannot happen in practicality and thus adjust to the societal system to sustain a normal life for themselves. This exactly confirms the idea of Indian feminism. Indian feminism is different in this sense that there is a struggle and resistance in different forms and yet there is some sort of belongingness and rootedness to one's culture and codes of conduct. In this context, Indian feminism departs from western concept of feminism which fights for equality and gender rights. Indian feminism advocates women for enlightenment and change at the same time keeping the values and ethics set by its culture.

Kapur's *A Married woman* thus deconstructs received understandings of sexuality, sex and gender in India and gives space for lesbian discourse. Like Raj Rao or Mahesh Dattani, she does not seem to support homosexuality but her approach has secular ideas. Her novels can be read as novels of protest against patriarchal norms, age old traditional beliefs and social codes that has no rationality and these notions are fractured or deconstructed. She seems to voice for a better living environment where every individual can gain respect in the society. Her novels throw light for betterment of society and mankind. Although she does not give any moral judgment, she addresses social concerns that need attention and rationality. In the text, we encounter Desire taking form in different characters for various things. Finally, the author's desire to spread awareness about marginalised sexual minorities and the desire to address this inequity needs praise. The text, thus, emphasises the reality of queer marginality and decenters heterosexuality as the standard norm.

The emergence of lesbian discourse is a threat to normative heterosexuality. Cheryl Clarke in, "Lesbianism, An Act of Resistance" comments:

> Women are kept, maintained and contained through terror, violence, and the spray of semen. Lesbianism is an ideological, political and philosophical means of liberation of all women from heterosexual tyranny. The Lesbian rejects male sexual/political domination, defies his world, his social organisation, his ideology, and his definition of her as inferior. The lesbian defines herself and rejects the male definitions of how she should feel, act, look, and live (128).

Kapur reiterates the notion where identity is a matter of conscious choice. Instead of fixed identity, we have now hybrid identities. Identity formation is never ending and is open ended rather than fixed and closed. So is Nina's life in *The Immigrant* which reinforces what the author intends to address.

Heterosexuality of women was seen as instrumental in perpetuating patriarchal oppression. Adrienne Rich, an American feminist in *Compulsory Heterosexuality and Lesbian Existence* argues that heterosexuality is not "natural" or intrinsic in human instincts, but an institution imposed upon many cultures and societies that render women in a subordinate situation. It was written to challenge the negligence of lesbian existence from a large amount of scholarly feminist literature. The text encourages heterosexual feminists to examine heterosexuality as a political institution which disempowers women and to change it. She argues that heterosexuality is a violent political institution making way for the "male right of physical, economical, and emotional access" to women. She urges women to direct their energies towards other women rather than men, and portrays lesbianism as an extension of feminism.

Adrienne Rich observes

> The assumption that 'most women are innately heterosexuals' stands as a theoretical and political stumbling block for many women. It remains a tenable assumption, partly because lesbian existence has been written out of history or catalogued under disease; partly because it has been treated as exceptional rather than intrinsic; partly because to acknowledge that for women heterosexuality may not be a 'preference' at all but something that has had to be imposed, managed, organised, propagandised and maintained by force is an immense step to take if you consider yourself freely and 'innately' heterosexual...... (119).

Astha's sexual encounters and her inability to fit into the accepted codes of gender behaviour signals Kapur's deconstruction of gendered identity. In *A Married Woman,* Kapur makes Astha at the end to be back with her heterosexual relationship, thus suggesting that there is no fixed destination where one can reach. Astha protests her subordination under patriarchy by choosing the 'abnormal' path. She makes her body as the site of resistance. She rejects heteronormative standard what every woman is expected to abide. Stability of identity is questioned. The title of the novel, *A Married Woman* which indicates heterosexuality as the stable norm is challenged. As Meenakshi Thapan writes:

> Both within and outside the family, women engage in the twin process of compliance and resistance, submission and rebellion, silence and speech, to assert their identities as women in what they clearly and assertively recognise as oppressive contexts and situation (170).

Summing Up

Mapping Kapur's Texts with the notion of Identity		
Diaspora Identity	Dislocation, Cultural transformation, state of in-betweenness, Hybridity	Nina & Ananda negotiate with cultural markers in *The Immigrant*
Self-Identity	Individual consciousness	Virmati in *The Difficult Daughters* and Sona, Rupa in *Home* discover

		their individual self
Cultural Identity	Cultural markers undergo change: name, clothes, food habits, beliefs. Identity gained through marriage and motherhood	Characters like Kasturi, Sona, Nina, Ananda, Ishita negotiate these tendencies
Sexual Identity	May not be stable. Decenters heterosexuality as the standard norm	Astha and Pipeelika in *The Married Woman*

3

Postmodern Feminism

3.1 Feminism

Feminism is a belief that women should have (economical, political and social) equality with men. Accordingly, it is clear that feminism is the belief that all people should be treated equally in legal, economic and social arenas, regardless of gender, religion, sexual orientation, ethnicity and other similar predominant identifying traits. The term Feminism has its origin from the Latin word 'Femina' meaning woman, and thereby refers to the advocacy of woman's rights, status and power at par with man on the grounds of equality of sex. Feminism refers to the advocacy of woman's right seeking to remove restrictions that discriminate against woman. The origin of feminism can't be traced through a single source, as it is located in numberless traditions. It is assumed that feminism originated from the French Revolution, in the drive for abolition of slavery and in the American Civil Right Movements. Feminism is a protest against the injustices against women. Various feminist movements in history have aimed to fight for equality with men, rights for women and against oppression and discrimination. The first voice in favor of woman's right was raised by Mary Wollstonecraft in *A Vindication of the Rights of Women* (1972). She demanded equal opportunities for women in the field of education, economics and politics. The strong male supporter of woman's liberation, John Staurt Mill, showed serious concern about woman's oppression in his *The Subjugation of Women* (1869). He felt the need for education for women empowerment and condemned woman's oppression as domestic slavery. Feminism may appear in different forms such as radical socialist, Marxist and so on but on the whole it is basically concerned with the question of identity. It is a movement to support the demand for equal, political and economic rights with men. Feminism is not meant to create awareness but to change the situation.

In the latter part of the eighteenth century, the Feminist Movement grew worldwide in 1960, and students, workers, blacks and women took part in it. Eminent feminists, who have played an important role in the woman's liberation movement, are Simone De Beauvoir (*The Second Sex* 1949), Betty Friedan (*The Feminine Mystique* 1963), Kate Millett (*Sexual Politics* 1969) and Germaine Greer (*The Female Eunuch* 1970).

No discussion of feminist writing can be complete without the mention of *The Second Sex.* Many of Beavoir's ideas such as the right to abortion/use of contraception for women, were elaborated by Kate Millet in *Sexual Politics*. The book also examines several myths, stereotypes and literary works and shows how these texts have helped to uphold misogynist, patriarchal ideals. In Kate Millet's *Sexual Politcs* (1970), the chief argument is that the differences between sexes are instituted by culture and not biology and the male domination is enforced through the institution of family, a major basis of patriarchy. Millet views gender politics as more predominant than class and argues that patriarchy limits women's chances of professional & intellectual growth. She reflects on how patriarchy uses violence to suppress women, as women are punished for prostitution, adultery and are denied the right to control their bodies through contraception and abortion. A key feature in Millet's work is that the theories of psychoanalysis, particularly those of Freud which she viewed, have been used as a propaganda against women.

Simone De Beauvoir, who established the principles of modern feminism in her book *The Second Sex*, comments that woman's position is not natural, but is a social construct. The concept of femininity is artificially shaped by customs and fashion, and man's dominance has been secured through ages by an ideological power. She defines feminism as:

> One is not born, but rather becomes, a woman. No biological, psychological, or economic fate determines the figure that the human female presents in society; it is civilisation as a whole that produces this creature, intermediate between male and eunuch, which is described as feminine. Only the intervention of someone else can establish an individual as another (295).

Simone De Beauvoir's famous statement "*One is not born, but rather becomes a woman*" clearly distinguishes sex from gender and suggests that gender is an aspect of identity gradually acquired. Sex is understood in terms of anatomy and biological performance; whereas gender has cultural meaning and form that body acquires and hence is unnatural. Gender is associated with cultural implications and performance depending on social and cultural codes in a given situation. Gender is a cultural construction and also a process of constructing ourselves. Gender and Sex are two different concepts. Sex refers to the biologically constituted form, whereas gender is assigned as per sex. Cultural, social, political and economic forces shape gender roles.

Simone De Beauvour in her book *The Second Sex* claims that feminity is processes in the society. She writes: "Throughout her childhood the little girl suffered bullying and curtailment of activity; but the less she felt herself to be an autonomous individual."

Simone De Beauvoir notes that

> ...the woman is defined and differentiated with reference to man and not he with reference to her; she is the incidental, the inessential as opposed to the essential. He is the subject, he is the Absolute – she is the other (313).

Simone de Beauvoir states "The terms masculine and feminine are used symmetrically only as a matter of form, as on legal papers" (345).

De Beauvoir in *The Second Sex* talks about economic independence, freedom and equality in work for women. Economic autonomy is what she wants for women. By the concept of 'other' she meant that women become agency for domestication, reproduction and procreation. De Beauvoir points out that lack of personal freedom within marriage has in turn dangerous consequences for women's identity as mother, because she then projects her marital frustrations on to her relations with her own children. She also points that women's desire to gain agency which is usually frustrated within the marital relationship, within the relationship that she has with her husband manifests itself through an excessive attempt to control her children, which again in itself is rather unhealthy.

Feminist theories question power structures, patriarchal norms and social practices that operate in society and subjugate women. It then designs strategies to eradicate such practices and aims for emancipation of women. This wave started in the 60s and 70s and in the present period the concept of 'otherness' has come about. Feminism also paved way for academic discourse on women, their marginal representation in literature and use of language. Feminism is resistance to these power structures and focus to liberate women from oppression and sexist aggression. Feminism is resistance to patriarchal power and it aims to struggle for equality for women. Julia Kristeva in her philosophical reverberation deconstructs all identities and binary oppositions. In literature, initially very few women wrote. And in doing so, they had to change their names and get it published. As Virginia Woolf clearly puts it "A Woman must have money and room of her own if she is to write fiction." (126).

Feminist critics like Elaine Showalter have introduced to writing, the feminist writing. 'Gynocriticism' coined by Showalter is a form of feminist criticism which restricts itself to the study of woman's writings and writings related to female experience. Elaine Showalter has shown three phases of woman's literature. The first phase she calls as 'feminine phase' where women writers had shown their women characters as heroines and ideal characters, self-sacrificing and enduring women who compromise in all situation for the welfare of families. The second phase is the 'feminist phase' where women show resistance and protest against dominance, patriarchal order, existing state of affairs and claim equal status in society. The third phase is the phase of self-discovery, introspection and question. Women had to face different problems in academic circles and in exposing their work of art. Today, the problems have minimized and women write to tell their ideas or make their writings as part of their activism.

In *Toward a Feminist Poetics*, Showalter traces the history of women's literature, suggesting that it can be divided into three phases. 1. Feminine 2. Feminist (1880-1920) 3. Female phase (1920 onwards). The first phase involves subordination and imitation of male agenda, the second phase is an act of protest and the third phase is attributed to autonomy and self-discovery. In this text, she coins the term 'gynocriticism' which refers to the 'study of women as writers'. Gynocriticsm comes as a result of critiques utilised under post structuralism and psychoanalysis schools of thought.

3.2 Postmodern Feminism

Postmodern feminism connects feminism and postmodern tenets. Postmodern feminists celebrate the notion of moving beyond the modernist polarities of liberal and radical feminism. These feminists use the ideas propagated by poststructuralism and deconstruction school of thought. Butler draws the idea of 'becoming' from Simone De Beavoir and reinvents the idea of gender in a deconstructive way. She talks about men and women as binaries and social categories. She gives a clear distinction between sex and gender and says that one would be born as male or female but gender identity, as a man or a woman are constructs of the society for convienience. We perform as per our gender codes and even our body behaves accordingly. Clothing, mannerism, speech and language are determinants in this performance. She opines that gender is a performance which is repetitive in order to be recognised. She equates gender as text, which is a process and refuses fixity of categories based on sex. The notion of gender as fixed is subverted and is seen as unstable. Stable identities and fixed concepts are challenged in the postmodern discourses. Postmodern feminism also rejects the assumption that all women share a common experience and oppression. They articulate that women cannot be framed in a single homogeneous group but one must be attentive to the differences which are inherent within. Feminism is a form of resistance to hegemonic power structures. Postmodernism and feminism, struggle against the 'grand narratives' such as patriarchy. Feminism takes the political position; where as feminist theory is rather philosophical and analytical approach to such issues. Postmodernist writings resist control mechanism, fixity, hierarchies and dominant discourses. Feminists of the recent period protest against the way social institutions supported by cultural values and normative expectations force women into an unreasonably narrow role. Some recent feminists, however, have preferred to develop an alternative to patriarchal discourse in the place of strategy of subversive writing. This is alternative/subversive writing.

Postmodern discourses postulate blurring boundaries and binaries and negating fixed categories. Postmodern feminist discourses inculcate the features of postmodernism and feminism to constitute a different approach and understanding of underlying issues within its framework. Postmodern feminists seek to analyse notions that bring gender inequality and seek to critique, deconstruct and subvert grand narratives that relegate women to the 'other'. Contemporary writing focuses on how things get misrepresented or do not find place in the main stream narratives, usually the focus being marginalisation and victimhood in terms of gender, sexuality, class and caste. The purpose of such literature is to examine the oppressive structures produced and regulated by grand narratives and canonical regime. Literature serves as a powerful discourse to shackle the canonical order and voice for the suppressed class. In postmodern feminist discourse, gender and sexuality is perceived through a new light. For example, Judith Butler and Lucy Irigaray argue that women's subordinate position is due to socio-cultural construct of gender.

Gender like identity is represented in a state of fluidity by many postmodern writers. In postmodern feminist thought, gender and sexual identities are looked upon as plural/fluid structures and challenge metanarratives like patriarchy, family and marriage that endorse heterosexuality. In this context, works of Kamala Das, Mahasweta Devi, Arundhati Roy, Manju Kapur, Bapsi Sidhwa need mention as their literary output has fierce voice of resistance and activism against the power monopoly which oppresses people based on caste, class, gender and sexuality. Texts like Mahasweta Devi's *Breast Stories*, Arundhati Roy's *God of Small Things*, Kamala Das's *My Story*, Indira Goswami's *The Moth Eaten Howdah of a Tusker* are testimonials of protest literature.

Poststructuralism and Deconstruction have close contiguities with postmodern tendencies. Anything having boundaries and of fixed nature is questioned. It resists fixity of definitions and classifications. Third wave feminism that began in the 1990s addressed plurality of experiences of women varying in class, race, colour etc. Postmodernism defers grand narratives/metanarratives; patriarchy being one of them. Lyotard says that grand narratives like Marxism, Christianity are macronarratives paving way for micronarratives. He also contests that the metanarratives are created and reinforced by power structures and hence they are also untrustworthy. Postmodern feminism addresses patriarchy as a dominant discourse, culturally and socially constructed ideology. Judith Butler brings a paradigm shift in the way gender was observed. She assigns gender as a construct. According to this theorist, we perform and enact the roles assigned to us. We perform and do it in our everyday actions and expressions. Butler challenges the constructed nature of gender identities. She relegates it to performance. Gender is a process of doing or becoming rather than simply being. It is so intensely ingrained in the minds that everything appears natural. We are incorporated within the gendered social framework from the moment of our birth. She explains that this dominant discourse imposes heterosexuality as the standard norm; making it seemingly appear natural. She questions various issues on body, sexuality and gender. Postmodern feminism considers process of production, reproduction, construction, reconstruction and deconstruction. Gender is not a static concept but is a dynamic process, a dynamic process sometimes informed by the biological identity.

Deconstruction is a way of reading a text, allowing the text to unravel multiple meanings. It encourages a kind of reading which would also peel away like an onion; the layers of constructed meaning. It questions the idea of fixed meaning and renders it as a meaning making process by itself. It allows the reader to search for the blind spots, the gaps to open new ways of thinking and interpretation. Postmodern feminism was greatly influenced by deconstructive thought. In that line of thought, Judith Butler regards gender as a text and a performance; the playing out of roles that has to be repeated and validated within specific social and cultural contexts. She also draws Simone De Beavoir famous statement, 'One is not born a woman, but rather becomes one'. Beauvoir in her *The Second Sex*, talks about the process of 'becoming' and 'othering'. Simone De Beauvoir, who established the principles of modern feminism in her book *The Second Sex*, comments that woman's position is not natural, but is a social construct. The concept of femininity is artificially shaped by customs and fashion, and man's dominance has been secured through ages by an ideological power.

3.3 Judith Butler

One of the pioneers of postmodern feminism is Judith Butler. She talks about gender identity and the term it implies. She regards gender as a performative construct. According to Butler, we not only simply belong to a gender, but rather we do our gender. She talks about the act of performing it. She terms gender as performance. Gender is usually seen to be integrally connected with two other terms – one is the body and the other is sexuality. Butler is also known for her activism for the lesbian and gay rights. Postmodern feminists assert that body, sexuality and gender are socially constructed and are seemingly natural heteronormative practices. For Butler, homosexuality is the earliest form and she revises Freud's interpretation of child's sexuality. According to Butler, gender incorporates not only our feminity or our masculinity, but also our sexuality and our stylised bodies which is socially constructed, rather than being natural. She talks about the constructed nature of gender identity and the notion of performativity. Gender or gendering is a process of doing or becoming rather than simply being. This tendency is so much internalised and naturalised that it appears to be seemingly normal. We are incorporated within the gendered social framework from the moment of our birth. Gender is a verb, a process of action, a process of production, reproduction, construction and reconstruction. Gender is a process of becoming as well as a process of unbecoming. It is not a static concept, rather a dynamic process – a dynamic process sometimes informed by the biological identity. *Gender Trouble* is one of the most powerful critique of heterosexual assumptions in feminist theory and of the dualism of masculinity and feminity. Butler also claims that language is also heavily gendered and this is the constructed quality of language and gender.

Butler challenges conventional notions of gender and develops her theory of gender performativity. The crux of Buter's argument in *Gender Trouble* is that the coherence of the categories of sex, gender and sexuality – the seemingly natural coherence is culturally constructed. She claims that sex is biological and gender is culturally constructed. According to her, gender like identity is unstable and not fixed. She questions the illusion of stable gender identity. She states that gender is performed and repeated in order to be recognised. Postmodern feminism, thus, connects to gender, body and sexuality. It questions the authority of grand narratives like patriarchy and subverts dominant discourses using poststructuralist thoughts and ideals especially that of deconstruction.

We find Butler using these ideas to redefine and reinvent her notion of gender. One is born as male or female based on the sexes but gender identity is ascribed by many constructs of society. She argues male and female are social and binary categories. Clothing, mannerism, language and roles are determined by societies based on these mechanisms. Gender consciousness or gendering is prevalent everywhere. Both men and women are caught under the oppressive mechanism of closed society but women succumb to it more. There is a pervasive gender consciousness that surrounds us and passes through traditions, beliefs, customs, myths and folk narratives. Judith Butler radicalises the conventional notion of gender identity by claiming that gender is performatively creative and there is no pre-existing gender identity. Butler understands gender, along with sex and sexuality, to be performative. Butler claims that gender is performatively created and there is no pre-existing gender identity. She states:

> There is no gender identity behind the expression of gender; that identity is performatively constituted by the very 'expressions' that are said to be its results. (*Gender Trouble* 34)

Postmodern feminism rejects the opinion that all women share a common experience/oppression. It claims that women cannot be seen as a homogeneous group. Even within one single country like India, problems faced by tribal women may be different from rural or urban region. Postmodern feminism is a kind of resistance to ways of thinking, perceptions and ideologies.

The hold of academia and other hegemonic groups(colonial powers, white educated males) got diluted with the emergence of a sophisticated Marxist criticism (along with other factors) which gave rise to contesting power groups and conflicting ideologies, so that the great traditions of a privileged category – 'Literature' – becomes a chorus of voices or 'literatures'. The rise of non-white feminisms, multicultural feminisms in the western context and the rise of Dalit (oppressed, downtrodden groups) literature and feminisms in the Indian context led to the foregrounding of new issues and new debates on identity, subjectivity and the role of language and culture. One of the core issues that these debates hinge on is the issue of difference. The concept of difference is defined by Julian Wolfreys as both "political and ontological," that "which makes possible any meaning or identity" since it derives from the "political and ontological necessity of recognising that different groupings (for example women, nonwhite and people of colour, gays and lesbians) not only differ from the white heterosexual norm, but also differ among themselves: women, for example, may be middle-class or working class, Black or Asian, straight or gay or bi, and/or any combination of any set of attributes" (Wolfreys, 2004). Thus, although many nonwhite theorists include "each other in shared analyses of oppression, and while most feminisms have aligned themselves with arguments against racism, xenophobia, and homophobia," (Guerin, et al, 2005) there is a strong protest against homogenisation of any kind. The issue of difference is a complex one since each minority group has its own issues and concerns, which, they argue, cannot be collapsed with those of others. The case of black feminists or 'womanists' can be furnished as an example of a differential framework. The use of the term womanist distinguishes feminists of colour; and the term was used by the writer Alice Walker to indicate a kind of feminism that does not always necessarily turn its back on the men of the same community.

Black feminists declare that their multiple oppressions put them in a different category to both white women as well as black men. They also feel that their interests and urgencies can be represented only by them. They draw on both essentialist and constructivist notions – so while they accept and celebrate their ethnic difference they simultaneously feel that "blackness" is culturally constructed as a sign of otherness in Anglo-American culture. The rich prose of writers like Alice Walker, Adrienne Rich and Maya Angelou also raises questions about their exclusion from the canon of American literature, or their half-hearted exclusion as a kind of tokenism. The interrogation of the canon by black women writers has led to the recovery and foregrounding of genres like autobiographies, slave and captivity narratives. Rich also talks about the "lesbian continuum" which is both about resisting heterosexuality and its politics (heteronormativity) and about the "woman-identified woman". Feminists like Walker offer a counter discourse to patriarchy by restoring a sense of the value of the maternal heritage in works like *In Search of Our Mothers' Gardens* (1983), *The Colour Purple* (1982) and critics like Barbara Smith formulate an alternative aesthetic in *Towards A Black Feminist*

Criticism (1977). In her work, Smith suggested a lesbian reading of Toni Morrison's *Sula* (1973) and of earlier works by American women authors.

Thus, it is noted that the concept of feminism has many variants. Firstly, the liberal feminism as advocated by Mary Wollstonecraft and then further taken by Betty Friedan and many others. This type of feminism advocates equal status at par with men in society. Radical feminism questions male hegemony and patriarchal oppression. To this category belong critics like Mary Daly, Kate Millet, Juliet Mitchel and others. Existential feminism advocates women to think, create space, identity and autonomy for themselves. Simone De Beauvoir represents this set of writers. Radical feminists were much more revolutionary compared to first wave feminists who confined only with equality in societal status. Radical feminists have ascertained that men use social system, practices and other performing acts of control to suppress women.

While the first wave feminism focused on suffrage and gender inequality, the second wave of feminism which started in the early 60s in United States and moved to other countries by 80s and 90s broadened their subject of concerns. Sexuality, family, custody and divorce laws, work place, reproductive rights, legal rights were all the subjects of discussion. Second wave feminism was more revolutionary in kind. Women should have control over their bodies and be protected against domestic violence are main objectives of this movement. Later in the 90s, post-structuralism and postmodern thoughts have influenced shaping feminist perceptions. The Third wave feminism is the recent one which realises that women are of many colors, ethnicities, nationalities and religion. Hence, they acknowledge diversity and study the problems differently. The earlier feminist movements addressed problems of the white women but the more recent ones embraced all the women. Third wave ideology focuses more on post-structuralism, interpretation of gender and sexuality. The influence of post structuralism was much observed in the third wave feminism. In the 80s and 90s the concept of 'otherness' and marginalisation is the prime concern. In postmodern feminism 'Body' becomes the site where identity formation begins.

Third wave theory usually incorporates elements of queer theory; anti-racism and woman-of-color consciousness; womanism; girl power; post-colonial; post-modernism; transnationalism; eco-feminism; individualist feminism; new feminist theory, transgender politics, and a rejection of the gender binary. The concept of feminism has taken a setback in the postmodern context. Postmodernism and the concept of feminism in the present context have similarities. Both ideologies challenge unitary definitions of truth. According to recent feminists, the consciousness of self is under constant change due to changing social conditions. Feminism as a totalitarian ideology itself is distorted by both feminists and post modernists. To decentre woman and bring in wider perception of looking at the different issues from variations of geography and culture becomes a significant move. Thus, to note this observation:

> Post modernism constitutes the expressing of a contextual discourse that problematises other discourses and thus enables us to critically examine the givens of other discourses. It exists thus as an alternative discourse to prevent a hegemonic domination of any one discourse (Salat 36).

Summing Up: Western Feminism

Feminist waves	Tenets	Important texts
1st wave feminism (19th & 20th century)	Liberal feminism of equality focused on legal issues. Right to vote, suffrage movement	John Staurt Mill 's *The Subjgation of Women* (1869) Mary Wollstonecraft's *A Vindication of the Rights of Women* (1742)
2nd wave (1950s & 60s)	Radical feminism, reproductive rights, education, legal and social rights	Simone De Beauvoir's *The Second Sex* (1949), Virginia Woolf, Betty Friedan's *The Feminine Mystique* (1963), Kate Millett's *Sexual Politics* (1969)

3rd wave (1990s)	Plurality of experiences. Race/colour/gender. Accommodated not just the problems of white women but third world countries. Feminist of color, consciousness raising, postructuralist interpretation of gender & sexuality, postcolonial & postmodern thinking	Julia Kristeva Judith Butler's *Gender Trouble: Feminism and Subversion of Identity* (1990)

Summing Up: Postmodern Feminism

- Resistance to power structures, hegemonies
  Male/female binaries as an artificial construct to maintain the power of the dominant group
- Rejects homogenous experience of all women
  Looks at multiplicities in experiences of women based on colour, class, caste, race, region
- Voiced for gay, lesbian and transgender rights
  Challenges heteronormativity

Theorists	Texts	Tenets
Simone De Beauvoir	*The Second Sex* (1949)	One 'becomes' a woman, the act of 'othering'
Elaine Showalter	*Towards a Feminist Poetics* (1979)	Feminine phase, Feminist phase, Female phase

Judith Butler	*Gender Trouble: Feminism and Subversion of Identity* (1990)	Gender is a signifier, process, social and cultural construct. Theory of performativity, Performative repetition of acts Questions compulsive gender performances
Julia Kristeva		Deconstructs all identities and binary oppositions. Intertextuality

3.4 Feminism in India

The feminist movements of the west definitely had some influence on woman's movement and emancipation in India. Indian feminism was concerned with the problems faced by Indian women in their various walks of life. Western feminism looked at identity, job equality and sexism; where as in India, it is the question of survival and resistance in a patriarchal set up where traditions, family and the society become oppressive mechanisms. Feminine is a set of culturally defined characteristics. Indian feminism is rooted with its culture. Jasbir Jain observes:

> Feminisms are several and they are culture-specific. The feminist discourse in India has, at times, gone all out to differentiate itself from the Feminisms of more affluent societies primarily, because of cultural reasons (81).

Indian feminists also fought against cultural issues within the patriarchal society such as inheritance laws and the practice of widow immolation known as Sati. Unlike the western feminist movements, Indian feminist movement was first initiated by men and later supported by women. Social reformers like Raja Ram Mohan Roy, Iswar Chandra Vidyasagar, and political revolutionaries like Mahatma Gandhi and Pandit Nehru wanted to liberate women from male tyrannical practices. Indian feminist movements aim for equality of sexes, property rights, right for education and a change in the existing order and equality for better system. Abandoning Sati, child marriage system, promoting legal rights to own property are chief concerns.

When we look at Indian history, we can see that women during the ancient times enjoyed supreme status. Women were worshiped in the form of goddess and the birth of girl child was considered as goddess Lakshmi coming to the house. Women had the right to choose their husband during 'Swayamwara' a practice where all eligible men gathered and the bride had to choose the one who wins the contest. This situation declined after the invasion of Muslim rulers in India. Fearing Muslim men picking women, the purdah system in which the entire body is covered came into existence. With that came the idea of child marriage, Sati and other inhuman practices. In the Manu's code of law for the society, women have an inferior status and are equated absolute property of men. During the 19th century, movements led by Raja Ram Mohan Roy and others aimed in uplifting such practices that devalued women. Roy, Iswar Chandra Vidyasagar, Rabindranath Tagore, Dayanand Saraswathi and few others voiced against inequality, discrimination, condition of widowed women and Sati system. Literature, therefore, has always been an effective vehicle for fundamental changes. To a large extent, the popularity of feminist ethics in India has also been generated by the image of 'New women' presented by literary writers in their works. The abolition of certain evil practices against women in the preceding centuries had also created a much-needed awareness in the society for imparting a better status to women. It was during the British rule in India that many relevant changes were made in order to ameliorate the pathetic condition of women. The Viceroy Lord William Bentik banned Sati in 1829. Social reformers like Raja Ram Mohan Roy had also supported this move. Similarly, remarriage of widows was sanctioned in 1856 and in 1929 a law was passed prohibiting child marriage. The most difficult task in India at that time was to educate women, because only a few women belonging to the families of zamindars were able to receive basic education. Many teachers, as well as social workers, considered it a necessity and started many educational institutions for women. In 1850s, Ishwar

Chandra Vidyasagar started many primary schools in the villages of Bengal. Arya Samaj, founded by Swami Dayanand, also propagated women's education. John Drinkwater Bethune established the first women's college in India in Calcutta in 1849. In 1851, Jotiba Phule came forward to educate the scheduled caste girls in Poona. Since then, there has been no looking back, as women also started clamoring for education for which they had been indifferent for ages. These attempts provided the much-needed impetus and Indian woman took a step towards social emancipation. Many great Indian women writers who appeared on the literary scene represented the educated group of Indian women. Toru Dutt, Cornelia Sorabji, Shevantibai Nikambe, Krupabai Santhianathan and Smt. Swarnkumari Ghosal are some of the prominent women writers of this time.

Later, during the Indian freedom struggle, inspired by Gandhian ideologies many women came out and freely participated in the political struggle. The constitution of India proclaimed in 1950 advocated women to have equal rights with men and all fundamental rights as given to men. Although legal rights, awareness and education have brought women in a much better level, yet even today in the age of development and modernity, we find cases in the society where women are subjected to oppression, female infanticide, dowry deaths, domestic violence, sexual exploitation, molestation, rape and even murder.

For Chamal Nahal, a noted Indian writer and critic

> I define feminism as a mode of existence in which the women is free of the dependence Syndrome. There is dependence syndrome whether it is husband, father, the community, or a religious group. When women will free themselves of the dependence syndrome and lead a Normal life, my idea of feminism materialises (17).

The vibrations of feminist movements were felt in the Indian soil as well. Veena Noble Dass describes:

> Feminism in Indian literature, particularly in Indian English writing is a by-product of the western feminist movement. But

> we cannot totally negate the contribution made by our freedom struggle, independence, spread of education, concern for economic development and stability, employment opportunities and above all the resultant new awareness of our women. As far as feminism is concerned regional literatures too fall in line with this pattern. The Indian women caught in the flux of tradition and modernity bearing the burden of the past and the aspirations of the future is the crux of feminism in Indian literature. A search for identity and a quest for the definition of the self, have become the prime features of women in literature under the sway of feminism (11).

Indian freedom movement and expansion of education brought in new awareness along with the influence of western feminist thought. The freedom movement led by Mahatma Gandhi had immense effect on the masses triggering the women folk also to step out of the domestic chores and equally participate in the freedom movement.

In the words of Surendra Narayan Jha in his *The Treatment of Modern Indian Woman in Manju Kapur's Difficult Daughters:*

> For the first time in Indian history, Gandhi's thought and actions gave new definitions to woman as an individual – independent and capable of taking care of herself. His invitation to women to participate in the freedom struggle as equal partners of men brought out of the conventional mode of behavior patterns prescribed in Manusmrati. To a writer, especially to the writers of the novels, the feeling aspect of this change of attitude to woman had a great significance (80).

The works of women writers in particular are significant in bringing in the new sense of political and social consciousness and in shaping the minds of young women in defining their roles and conduct. R. K. Dhawan acknowledges the importance of feminism in the Indian English fiction:

> Feminism has echoed in the Indian English fiction too. The existential struggle to establish one's identity, to assert one's individuality and fight to exist as a separate identity appears in the novels of Indian women novelists. We find the fullest

> expression of women problems in the novels of Kamala Markandaya, Anita Desai, Ruth Prawer Jhabvala, Nayantara Sahgal and Shashi Deshpande; and also in the novels of younger generation of women novelists namely Gita Mehta, Shobha De, Jai Nimbkar, Githa Hariharan and others (22).

Recent generation women novelists have brought to the front their concerns for the fair sex and the related issues pertaining to women down the ages. Through their characters, these writers are able to bring in a sense of awareness and consciousness. This is resonated in R. K. Dhawan's *Feminism and Recent Indian Literature-*

> The rise of feminism has spurred writing women who give expression to their own experiences and feelings. In feminist studies, women are both the, "subjects and objects" of study. Interestingly, women have appropriated the right to define, to give meaning to interpret, a right that had been exclusively male ever since the creation of knowledge.
>
> Literature reflects not only the social reality but also shapes the complex ways in which men and women organise themselves, their personal relationships and their perception of the socio-cultural reality. Indian novelists have dealt with family relationships with high seriousness because the tradition of India gives great importance to the family unit. They have extensively dealt with the theme of man-woman relationship which has a great historical, sociological and cultural significance (29).

Male writers too have advocated the cause of woman's emancipation. R. K. Narayan's women characters are of two types. One group belongs to the conventional and traditional mind set; while the other group strives for freedom from strict social practices. Bhabhani Bhattacharya's women characters, on the other hand, in some way or other are integral to the development of plot. Although these characters too are under patriarchal pressure, yet they are positive and have strength to face challenges with positive mindset. These writers do not directly deal with feminist issues but convey the idea of the need for woman's emancipation. Women writers on the other hand consciously or unconsciously wrote on subjects related to the woman's world. This may be so because being a woman themselves, they could relate easily to the experiences and fictionalise the same. Anita Desai presents violence and tyranny faced by women and their disturbed psyche. The inner turmoil and neurotic behavior becomes her prime concern. Loneliness, helplessness, depression form the characteristic traits of her women characters. Desai's women characters are escapists who do not attempt to face challenges and reality with positive outlook but are sensitive, lack strength and courage and hence commit suicide or take extreme steps. Ruth Prawar Jhabwala has portrayed both the traditional Indian women with conventional and stereotyped thoughts and also the modern educated women with liberal views. Her fiction is not directed towards feminism as much of her concern is on east/west encounter and cultural conflicts. Kamala Markandaya through her female protagonists has shown that all problems faced by women are due to the financial dependence and hence women should have economic independence and this will minimize the existing problems faced by women. But she has not pointed out to areas like how social conditioning and environment, sexual discrimination and so on are also responsible for the existing status of women. Shobha De writes about the lives of urban aristocratic women. Her women marry for money, power, social status and sexual satisfaction. They are modern, educated, glamorous and ambitious; strive for self-identity but lack ethics and morality. De's elite women have neither family attachment nor bonding with anyone nor any values but crave for money, success and social status. The author's woman's world is of a very small section of the society who belong this elite class. Although Indian women want to achieve independence and individuality, they do not do so at the cost of family and marital bonds. Marriage, familial bonds and the values associated with it are some things that Indian women normally hold as their priority. Shashi Deshpande's fiction stands apart in her delineation of female characters. She vividly depicts the social realities of Indian life and mirrors Indian womanhood. She points that women should overcome their weaknesses and should be assertive. She writes from a feminist perspective and aims for social change through reinterpretation and revaluation of woman's status in the society. She appeals to all Indian women and not restricts herself to a particular section. Indian English fiction by women writers has captured feminine consciousness and sensibilities. Female subjectivity is the much-explored theme in many of their writings. Thus, writers like Kamala Markandaya, Nayantara Sahgal, Anita Desai, Geetha Hariharan, Shashi Deshpande, Kiran Desai and Manju Kapur and many more have left an indelible imprint on the readers of Indian fiction in English. Sushila Singh's remark in this context is justified.

> ...the concept of feminism raises fundamental questions about reading, writing, and the teaching of literature. Feminism has transformed the perceptions of life and literature. It operates as an interdisciplinary tool for social and cultural analysis and as political practice. Literary theorists believe that feminist theory or criticism does not denote simply the addition of new subject matter to an existing system of knowledge. By adding women to literature, feminist criticism helps to expose the incompleteness of what once seemed universal. Therefore, a rethinking on the whole critical enterprise becomes necessary (2).

Thus, we can note that women writers addressed various issues but chiefly pertained to the lives of women. Consciously or unconsciously they touched upon feminist ideologies in their writings. A re-examination of ideas, perceptions and critical enquiry to stereotypes came into existence with the emergence of women writers in English. The present day writers re-visit the past, re-interpret and make bold attempts to question the canonical order, thus carving a niche for themselves through creative works.

3.5. Gender and Sexuality

Manju Kapur's writings also reveal her major concerns for the female gender. Her protagonists strive to free themselves from traditional rigid practices and look for freedom and independence in domestic and family structures. She is no doubt one among the many who has displayed a mature understanding of the female psyche and shown valid concerns to gender issues by fictionalising ground realities. In her fiction, she has shown the problems faced by women in general. In one of her interviews, she says – "My novels also center on women. It's about how women negotiate with the outside world." (web.thehindu@thehindu.co.in.com).

Her fiction centers on family issues, husband-wife relation, the role of women in the family and the tussle between modern and traditional concepts. Her female characters are caught in a trap between tradition and modernity. They yearn for personal choice and freedom and at the same time want to preserve familial bonds and relationships. This dichotomy makes them to compromise for the sake of domestic harmony. And this is how Indian feministic perception varies. Western feminist thoughts do have impact on the Indian minds but with a difference. Family, relations, values, practices and ethics are so rooted to the Indian mind that western ideologies do not get synergised here.

Much often Kapur was compared to Jane Austen for her meticulous detailed presentation of family and married lives of women. During an interview, when she was asked how she felt being compared to Jane Austen, her reply was –

> I love being compared to Jane Austen, this is such a compliment – but unfortunately, I don't think it is true. First of all, she was a genius and I am not. Secondly her canvas is a narrower one than mine. But yes, there is one thing in common – and probably one shared by a lot of women writers – addressing larger social, economic and gender issues through the prism of the family (http://randomhouseindia.in).

Kapur's *Difficult Daughters* is a tale of women of three generations and their perception towards various norms set in the Indian society against the backdrop of Indian freedom struggle. The novel at length talks of female desire, passion, compromise and compliance. The lives of Kasturi, representing the traditional women, Virmati, the central character representing revolt and protest against patriarchal set ups and her daughter Ida, as the modern woman is portrayed in various forms. Kapur's women belong to the three phases as put forward by Elaine Showalter. Virmati's mother Kasturi becomes the conventional woman who restricts herself to traditions; whereas Virmati becomes the second generation of women who protest and revolt against traditional practices and are progressive and forward looking. While at the backdrop, the country is fighting for freedom, so is Virmati struggling for independence of personal self and from the shackles of tradition bound society. Again, in the same novel, we have the Professor's wife Ganga, who remains unnamed for quite a few number of pages thus indicating the lack of self-identity and belonging to the conventional sort of women who firmly believe and accept that men have control on their lives.

In all of Kapur's novels, we have these three different types of women as put forward by Elaine Showalter under different phases. Kapur juxtaposes two types of women: the conventional and the revolting women. Virmati, Astha, Nina, Nisha, Ishita are all initially portrayed as the conventional types who confine themselves to the roles of mothers, daughters and wives, but gradually they realise their needs, revolt in order to have space for themselves and become assertive enough to voice their opinions. This transition is clearly shown in Kapur's women characters.

In her second novel, *The Married Woman*, Astha, the central character struggles to establish her identity and individuality by questioning the canon of social codes set for women. In all of Kapur's fiction, be it Virmati, Astha, Nina or Nisha, these female protagonists learn to protest and have their way. They protest within the family set-ups for autonomy and be part of social activism and raise their voice. Commenting on Kapur's works, Malti Agarwal says:

> Like many other Indian women writers, she voices the trials and tribulations of her female characters who, no doubt, recognise the primal essence of family bond but are conscious of their individuality. While living in the suffocating atmosphere of the traditional values of middleclass constraints, Kapur's heroines – Virmati, Astha and Nisha, all strive to assert themselves (26).

Kapur makes her women characters participate in outside agenda as social activists and at home to rebel and raise voice against patriarchy. Swarnalata in *Difficult Daughters* and Astha and Pipeelika in *A Married Woman* participate in social movements to create awareness in the society. Making women participate in outside environment is a strategy that Kapur skillfully uses to suggest the need for protest against social ostracism.

In her third novel, *Home*, child sexual abuse, the problems of infertility and the related harassment faced by women are beautifully sketched by Kapur. Families yearning for the boy baby and the girl child's responsibility at the domestic chores are well portrayed, all these forming the bulk of Indian psyche. Women suffer at different stages of lives and their inner turmoil manifests often in the form of headaches as in case of Virmati, Astha, Shugun and for Nisha, it is the skin problems. Her severe skin condition is the external manifestation of the burden and mental conflicts that she undergoes. Nina in *The Immigrant* is free from Indian patriarchal regimes but she lands in different problems in her diaspora existence.

One striking observance in all of Kapur's fiction is how the father figures or the male counter parts are supportive for the cause of women and the need for higher education and economic independence. In this sense, Kapur does not altogether write from a feminist standpoint but perhaps tries to surface that the notions of gender determined roles have so deeply penetrated in a woman's psyche especially of the older generation that everything seems natural and correct. An older woman tries to teach and perpetuate this gender consciousness into younger women whereas the male counter parts are shown supportive in certain respects. Perhaps there is a plea for women to have more liberal views and show concern for other women as well. Father figures in Kapur's fiction are supportive of daughter's education. They encourage them. Virmati's father, Astha's, Nisha's, understand that education provides not only better match in marriages but also gives them economic independence. Kapur has not only shown how women are being exploited in a patriarchal society by rigid laws and customs, socialisation of gender ethos but she has also pointed how women are subject to subordination by women themselves who may be mothers, mother in law or sisters. In *Home*, all these relationships between women are portrayed and, in most situations, it is men who support the women. So, in some sense Kapur challenges feminist literature. Men in her fiction encourage female education and are much more supportive. The mothers teach their daughters to abide by the rules set up in patriarchy, the mothers in law are authoritative and like to impose power and so on. Husband and wife antagonism is discussed at length by Anita Desai, Kamala Markandaya and other male writers as well. But Kapur has shown a much more balanced outlook by both the partners.

Gender is one important markers of identity and it is also subject to the problem of identity. One may belong biologically to a particular sex, but there are cultural and social issues that transform sex to gender thereby making it a complicated term. The male gender is expected to be rational, active, strong and courageous, the attributes associated with masculinity in a patriarchal social set up; where as the female gender is inclined to being meek, soft, passive, and emotional and the gender identities get constructed with these perceptions. Gendering is a social process and hence a social construct. In a patriarchal environment, what defines a woman is not the anatomy but also the social conditioning which influences and moulds her psyche to achieve the traditionally accepted feminine roles. Kate Millet in her seminal book *Sexual Politics*, defines gender as a, "Personality, structure in terms of sexual category" (3).

Judith Butler radicalises the conventional notion of gender identity by claiming that gender is performatively creative and there is no pre-existing gender identity:

> There is no gender identity behind the expression of gender; that identity is performatively constituted by the very "expressions" that are said to be its results (34).

Gender classification occurs from birth and continues throughout one's lifetime. Girls are expected to be cooperative, compassionate, enduring; whereas boys are socialised towards independence, assertiveness and achievement. Men belong to the public world and women to the private spheres. Such social conditioning since the tender age gets internalised that it almost becomes natural.

In *Home*, Nisha's mother Sona teaches her daughter about how she should behave or keep herself to societal expectations.

When Raju, Nisha's younger brother goes out to play, Nisha insists:

> "I want to go too."
>
> "You can't;" said mother shortly.
>
> "Why? Why can't I?"
>
> "It is better for girls to remain inside"
>
> "Why?"
>
> "You will get black and dirty...you will look like sweeper woman who comes to the house. You want to look like a kali bhainsi?"
>
> ...
>
> "Now how can you be like me if you get dirty and black playing in the sun? Who will want to marry you?" (Home 51-52)

According to the family members, Nisha being a 'manglik' needs to pray and fast for better prospects in getting married. As Simon De Beauvoir comments:

> The mother, as we shall see, is secretly hostile to her daughter's liberation, and she takes to bullying her more or less deliberately; but the boy's effort to become a man is respected, and he is granted much liberty. The girl is required to stay at home; her comings and goings are watched: she is not encouraged to take charge of her own amusements and pleasures. It is unusual to see woman organise by themselves a long hike or an excursion on foot or by bicycle, or devote themselves to games such as billiards or bowling (358).

Empathy, tolerance and virtue are qualities associated with womanhood and the Indian mythological figures bear testimony to this. These narratives very often become a source of inspiration or benchmark for Indian women to pass on these qualities to their daughters who would soon become wives and mothers. Sona is worried when at the age of sixteen Nisha is not able to peel the potatoes or cut the ginger quickly. Sona expresses her conventional outlook: "This is the life of a woman: to look after her home, her husband, her children, and give them food she has cooked with her own hands." (Home 126)

Sona wants traditional upbringing for Nisha who can excel in domestic chores. She makes Nisha perform pujas and makes her listen 'Vat Savitri Katha' and says to her,

> "See, this is what you must be like." (Home 133)

> "How are you going to get married, madam if you do not make sacrifices?" "I don't want to marry." mumbles Nisha. "Who will look after you if you don't marry? (Home 92)

Sona gets violent when she finds Nisha had cut her long hair in the parlour. Her skin conditions make the situation worse for her. Against all these odds, Nisha emerges as women of strength. She requests her father Yashpal; "If only you could take with you, Papaji," she pleaded in a rush, "I have seen girls working in shops. Why should it be only Ajay, Vijay and Raju? There must be something I too can do" (Home 267).

She pleads: "Give me a chance to show you what I can do" (Kapur: 287). She pleads her father "I know I can do a better job, please Papaji, please, if you could help Rupa Masi why can't you help me?" (Home 285).

In this context, Mary Wollstonecrafts's statement is justified.

> Woman are told from their infancy, and taught by the example of others that.... softness of temper, outward obedience and a scrupulous attention to a puerile kind of propriety will obtain for them the protection of man... (21).

Home becomes a metaphor of meaning. In her own home, Nisha is not comfortable because of the sexual abuse she faced in her childhood and had to leave to her aunt's house. Home is being left to move to a house. Then towards the end of the novel, we find that although Nisha struggles and emerges as a successful business woman, her life turns to the same conventional trap of getting married and bearing children. She is trapped again in the concept of home which represents the idea of woman, wife and mother. Kapur seems to suggest that life is a vicious circle and however hard we try, life takes us back to the roots. And for a woman, it is not that so simple. Kapur's protagonists fight against all odd situations, question traditional norms and become assertive but at some circumstance they have to settle to conventional mode of life. The title *Home* emphasises the inseparable connectivity between women and home. It subverts the idea of home when the protagonist is 'not at home' because of a horrific incident of child sexual abuse. For Nisha, her aunt's home is home to foster freedom, education, reason and equality; whereas her own home becomes a site of oppression, gender power and regulating people's lives under patriarchy and tradition. Home also becomes a site of woman's subordination and oppression but Kapur's protagonist makes it a site of struggle and conflict to assert her right and make space for her life.

Kapur's mother characters like Kasturi in *Difficult Daughters*, Astha's mother in *A Married Woman*, Sona in *Home* and Nina's mother want their daughters to follow traditional practices, values and prepare for ideal womanhood as the scriptures portray. But the daughters in doing so revolt and question the conventional norms.

Virmati's mother Kasturi holds traditional norms and values so much and believes that for a woman, marriage and childbearing is the foremost obligation. For her "A Woman's shaan is in her home… a woman without her own home and family is a woman without moorings…" (*Difficult Daughters* 111, 115)

Kapur subtly deconstructs some relationships within the family system. Motherhood is celebrated and myths about mother as dignified figure, the selfless, starving one who feeds the rest of the family and is the last to eat the remains, were celebrated and portrayed in most fiction, early and the present. But Kapur attempts to subvert this conventional image of motherhood. Kasturi in *Difficult Daughters* uses all methods and resorts to the use of twig for elimination of god's blessing 'the will of God' (9) from her body. Kasturi, although having a very traditional mind set submits herself to patriarchy and is forced by the situations to go against the norms of society.

The concept of motherhood is again subverted in *Custody*, where the children are at stake and we have the heroine plunging into the arms of another man for her personal needs. Mother usually is seen as role model. But in *Difficult Daughters*, Ida pronounces, "the one thing I had wanted was not to be like my mother" (1). The mother-daughter relationship is usually supposed to be empathetic, compassionate and friendly approach between the two. But this approach takes a different turn in Kapur's fiction. The concept of motherhood is challenged. The concept of motherhood is questioned when in *Home*, Kapur juxtaposes two sisters – Sona and Rupa, both of whom are unable to conceive even after years of marriage. But Sona is anxious and too concerned about the matter; whereas Rupa is much easy with it. When Sona discloses her news of preganancy to Rupa: "Rupa received the information much stoically. Her mind leaped to the little baby in her sister's arms" (Home 32).

And then:

> She was now supplying pickles and sweet chutneys to local restaurants as well as shops, and had hired a woman to help her. She wished to own a car, she wished to go on more holidays, and above all, she wished she had enough money to buy out the tenant who was causing her husband and father-in-law much tension. More than an elusive baby, Rupa focused her attention on financial success (*Home* 32).

Rupa and her husband are fine with their status of not able to bear a child and they are able to adjust well to a society which usually condemns women who are infertile. So, Kapur shows the differences in responses by two sisters who suffer from the same disorder. Sona has to bear all the taunts from her mother-in-law because she could not bring enough dowry and also not able to bear children. But unlike Desai's women characters, Sona creates her own space in her home, ignores the comments received and her patience bears fruit in the form of a daughter and a son years later. Sona and her daughter Nisha are the two women characters who are majorly discussed. Sona has troublesome life under the shadow of her mother-in-law and when Nisha grows, Sona wants her daughter not to aim for further education but learn domestic chores to become a good wife and daughter-in-law. Mothers often become the agents of patriarchal values. Daughters, on the other hand, resist this patriarchy, thus calling into question the smooth relation between mothers and daughters and also the power politics of elder women on the younger ones.

One of the key concerns of Kapur in *Home* is how gender operates within the framework of joint family system. Men for the public domain and women for the private sphere are enforced in the Banwarilal's patriarchal family system. The family members are so deeply rooted in the family way of life that everything is usual and unquestioningly follow tradition and practices. But the grandchildren of the patriarch question and challenge some of the established codes that operate within the family system. Arranged marriage system, acceptance of dowry, and the values of living together, women being engrossed with the domestic chores are some stereotyped traditions strongly accepted and followed in *Home.* The family witnesses a funeral in the form of Sunita's death (Banwarilal's daughter). But it was only him and Yashpal who went for the cremations and "the women stayed at home as was appropriate". Kapur has emphasised that home and women are something unseparable and deeply connected in Indian families.

Kapur has clearly shown that patriarchy brings woman's subordinate position and oppression in home and society. This begins with the idea of gender. Gender regulates the thinking processes, behavior, conduct and laws. Gender concept is universal. However, there are differences with respect to how each society or culture marks, depicts or manifests gender. Mary Klages, Associate Professor, University of Colorado points out that gender is constructed through "binary oppositions that ... divide the world into male and female and valuing male over female" (12). The male/female binary opposition is questioned by postructuralist school of thought.

Kapur shows how both men and women are victims of social norms and traditions which deprive them from freedom of choice. According to Radha Chakravarthy,

> Gender issues are central to Kapur's worldview in the lines of the female figures; we encounter questions about marriage, motherhood, woman's work in and out of the home, the body, sexuality, the different forms of violence against women ranging from emotional blackmail to dowry deaths and sexual abuse (119).

Women are stereotyped and subordinated in the roles assigned to them and are subject to male violence. Kapur's fiction explores the identities of women with respect to the roles assigned to them: wife, mother, daughter that are conditioned by not only class and education but rooted in Indian mind set.

Marriage also becomes an integral part in women's lives. In all of the novels, how mothers and fathers are too concerned about their daughter's wedding is portrayed. In patriarchal societies, girls are considered liabilities and after their marriage, a big responsibility becomes off the shoulders. In *Home*, Sona is too concerned about her daughter's looks and dressing. She sets tone for her daughter's marriage by considering 'it was time that clothes were engaged to do their job properly, to set off her looks, as hers were done..." (*Home* 136). After marriage, the next task that lay is to produce children to make the generation continue. Hence, male child is heartily welcomed. Kapur highlights the truths of miserable lives of young women who fail to reproduce and are subject to humiliation in society especially by women themselves. Indian families are more often obsessed with bearing male child. Kapur is conscious to note this fact. In *A Married Woman*, Astha is surprised when her US returned husband Hemant says:

> I want to have my son soon; I want to be as much a part of his life as papaji is of mine." He continues "Of course, we will have a son, and if we don't we needn't stop at two (*A Married Woman* 61).

When Sona is unable to conceive even after ten years, her situation became worse. Every gesture of the mother-in-law suggested that "the daughter-in-law had no right to exist, and if she had to live, why in their house? Only when the men came home at night was there the semblance of a caring family" (*Home* 11). Kapur has concerns for the marginalised group: women and children. Most of her novels have a touch of bildungsroman effect where there is conscious effort to portray the psyche of a young girl child and how it matures to understand and adapt to a situation. Thus, the lives of young children too are much of her concern. Her latest novel, *Custody* is the story describing the fractured bond of marriages and the lives of suffering children at the hands of divorced parents. The author in *Home* as well as *Custody* shows how often a childless marriage is despised and the blame put on women irrespective of where ever the problem is. The impact of infertility is terribly realised by Ishita while going through a medical treatment in a hospital as:

> Smaller than the ants on the ground, smaller than the motes of the dust in the sunlit air, smaller than drops of dew caught between blades of grass in the morning, was Ishita as she sat in the gynecologist's office with her mother-in-law (*Home* 24).

In *Home*, Kapur again emphasises the Indian mindset of craving for male child.

> All the members of the family want Astha to bear a boy baby. Special pooja was offered to Gods to grant them a boy. Hemant, says that they would keep trying until a baby boy is born. As expected, Astha gave birth to a son and the whole family was very pleased and Astha is satisfied and relieved as "she had partaken of the archetypal experiences marked out for the female race (69).

Women are taught by other women to carry forward the tradition. Sona wants her daughter to learn how to cook, pray for a future husband and show excellence in domestic chores. It is only Nisha's aunt Rupa who educates her. Rupa and her husband Prem Nath are shown in contrast with others. They represent a class who embrace realities and are much more sensible. If child bearing proves futile, they find happiness in business and in nurturing Nisha. Rupa and her husband symbolise reason, acceptance and go beyond gender myths. They rise above gender constrains.

Kapur's women like Kasturi, Virmati, Ganga, Nisha are powerless in patriarchal set-up but are powerful when it comes to oppressing other women, mostly their daughters. This is the paradox of power struggle within patriarchy. Kapur shows beautiful expression of women's world of the conventional old order with engaging food lexical.

Kasturi in *Difficult Daughters* broods about what it means to qualify for a woman:

> With all the breads, she could make, puris with spicy gram incisive, luchis big as plates, Kulchas, and white and long, tandoori rotis, layers of flaky flour, paranthas, crisp and stuffed. With morrabas, never soggy, and dripping juicy sweet. With seasonal pickles of lemon, mango, carrot, cauliflower, turnip, red chillies, dates, ginger, and raisins. With sherbets of khas, roses and almonds, with hot and cold spiced milk and sweet. With barfis made of nuts and grains soaked overnight, and ground fine between two heavy stones. With sweets made of thickened milk. With papad, the sweet ones made out of ripe mango, the sour ones with raw mango, and the ones to be fried with dal and potato. With thread spun, with cloth woven, with durries, small stitched carpets, phulkaries, with pyjam kurtas, shirts, and salwar kameezes (*Difficult Daughters* 57-58).

Kasturi is glad that her mother taught her roles in the kitchen. Kapur's detailed description needs praise.

> All of a sudden Kasturi felt grateful to her mother for those long hours she has spent in kitchen, cutting, peeling, chopping,

> slicing, pounding, wrapping, mixing, kneading, baking, roasting, stirring and frying (deep plus shallow) It paid to know these things (188-189).

Kapur has a balanced approach. She has a feminist approach but she is not a feminist altogether. She portrays the realities that surround the lives of men and women. According to her, both men and women struggle under the oppressive mechanism of a closed society and women are prone to at a larger extent. Kapur skillfully shows how the constructed nature of gender operates in every sphere of our lives and both men and women are bound by this pervasive gender consciousness. Woman's oppressive status is due to patriarchy, traditional beliefs and practices, our ancient myths and folk tales that draw codes for women and women themselves who blindly want other women to follow patriarchal codes of conduct.

Kapur's women characters because of all these oppressive forces, at times, suffer from psychological traumas. This gets manifested in the form of headaches and skin diseases as in the case of Nisha in *Home*. But these women learn to strike a balance their lives, fulfill their needs without letting down family and the related expectations. They emerge as bold, assertive and approach life with positivism. Kapur is a sincere crusader for women's education as it leaves space for rational thinking, liberty and economic independence. Kapur reiterates Simone de Beauvoir: "economic independence and liberation from orthodox traditions of society" (126).

Kapur's women protagonist come from well to do families and are educated. Although her heroines strive to aspire for independence and identity, yet they cannot gain full control over their self. This is because of their duty consciousness towards family and children. They tend to deviate, but return to compromise to fulfill the needs of the family. Kapur shows that for Indian women family is the first priority. She cannot achieve complete self as for her 'self' means family as well.

Kapur wants the society to awaken, rethink and be sensible. This is voiced through instances like: Aijaz being portrayed as a secular and broadminded Muslim who is associated with a theater group which works for societal awakening. Aijaz becomes a cult representing social awareness. Theater symbolises the act of showing the realities and Aijaz uses theater to bring in awareness. Kapur too shows us through different characters the various realities that need reinterpretation. Kapur is social activist and she voices her concerns through literature. Some characters are also activists. In *Difficult Daughters,* Swarna Lata is a feminist and political activist, participating in freedom struggle. The author voices her concern in *Difficult Daughters* that "Society would be better off if its females were effective and capable" (163). Astha in *A Married woman* emerges as an activist through her participation in the social agenda.

Manju Kapur voices through her protagonist, Astha in *A Married Woman*:

> A woman should be self-controlled, strong willed, self-reliant and rational, having faith in the inner strength of womanhood. A meaningful change can be brought only from within by being free in the deeper psychic sense (*A Married Woman* 6).

A strain of despair and disillusion is predominant in these novels. Manju Kapur feels that, "A meaningful change can be brought only from within by being free in the deeper psychic sense" (*A Married Woman* 101).

4

Conflicts and Resolution

This chapter throws light on the various conflicts as addressed in Kapur's fiction through various characters and situation. Conflicts between self/individuality and society, emotion and rationality, desire vs. commitment, conflict between mother and daughter and dichotomy between tradition and modernity and the consequent impact on social values and ethics are well discussed in her novels. Although Kapur does not seem to advocate or make any direct comments, yet a close reading of her fiction reveals her sense of concern for social issues. Her fiction displays the need for change in thinking, and mental makeup and the role of education for women empowerment for the betterment of mankind and society at large. Women's empowerment as Kapur points out in her fiction can be defined in terms of achieving power in order to take part in decision making, designing their lives, influencing the social and political process. The chapter emphasises the conflicting situations and how each character responds to these situations.

There are various conflicts, frictions and imbalances that Kapur addresses in her fiction. One such is the mother-daughter relationship. Although both belong to the same gender, there is some friction between the two.

4.1 Conflict in Familial Bonds

The mother-daughter relationship is not smooth. They often encounter friction in relationship and this could be because of the conflicts between tradition and modernity. The image of motherhood is dismantled. Mother in the patriarchal Indian society teaches her daughter the values of home, family, children and the need for the presence of authoritative male figure in the family. Each of Kapur's women pass on these ideals to their daughters, hence women are considered the torch bearers of tradition, values and customs in a family and society. Mothers in patriarchal society condition their girl child at the young age to adapt and adopt the norms set up in the existing society. This creates a rift between the mother and the daughter because one imposes and the younger generation opposes. This conflict between the two causes maternal alienation. Maternal indifference, lack of support, sympathetic approach and concern for the girl child within the family system affects harmonious existence and hence most women characters search for love and bonding outside the family. Hence, family also becomes a site for oppression.

Kasturi fails to understand Virmati's thirst for love. Ida tells the readers:

> At times Virmati yearned for affection, for some sign that she was special. However, when she put her head next to the youngest baby, feeding in the mother's arms, Kasturi would get irritated and push her away. 'have you seen to their food-milk-clothes-studies?' (DD 6)
>
> Years later when Ida rebuilds Virmati's story from the information provided by her relatives she can still sense that: 'The language of feeling had never flowed between them' (DD 11).

Lack of sympathy and concern makes Virmati, drift towards Harish. The illicit love that she enters into is because of the lack of understanding at home. In *A Married Woman*, Astha's entry into the lesbian relationship is again because of lack of love and concern from her husband. Nina in *The Immigrant* gets involved into extramarital relation because of husband's lack of time, love and concern. The author seems to plead that a family structure should be that of love, understanding and bonding and doing so will give harmonious existence.

O.P. Dwivedi writes about *Difficult Daughters* as:

> The novel covers three generations of daughters starting from Virmati's mother, Kasturi, Virmati and ending with Ida. Each of these daughters never share a happy relationship with their respective mothers and always remain alienate. Their daughterhood has spelt dooms for their mother (32).

4.2 Conflict between Tradition and Modernity

Tradition is deeply rooted in any society. Since ages traditions, practice and beliefs are integral part of Indian societies. Both men and women are bound by this tradition and for women it is extended further because women are supposed to be the torch bearers of tradition and culture. Mothers pass the tradition to the younger ones in the family. Virmati, Nisha, Nina and Astha are told by their mothers to perform and behave according to the dictation of the society. Clara Nubile in *The Danger of Gender* observes:

> In modern India the situation is still far from an ideal, liberated, democratic model. Indian women keep on struggling against the burden of tradition, against the legacy of the past and the orthodoxy of patriarchal system (271).

Kasturi in *Difficult Daughters* embodies tradition. Whatever she speaks or does is within the jurisdiction of traditional set up. According to Kasturi, marriage, family and to look after one's husband is the prime duty of every woman. Kapur's fiction shows two types of women. In most of her novels, contrasting women characters are presented. One set of women who belong to older generation are conventional, passive and tradition bound. This set of women firmly believes in the patriarchal system, remain submissive and are conscious about their familial roles as daughters, wives and mothers. The only occasions where they appear powerful are when they try to impose these traditional virtues on their female children. To this group belong women like Kasturi and Ganga in *Difficult Daughters*, Sona in *Home* and Astha's mother. The other set of women belong to younger generation, are much educated and are career oriented. These women accept tradition and do practice them but they do not do so blindly. They question stereotypes and go against practices which have no logical connection. Virmati,

Astha, Nina, Nisha and Shagun are rebellious, bold and seek freedom from traditional bondage. Mothers, thus, become symbols of oppressive agents of patriarchy and daughters become the forces of resistance. The older women represent silence and younger women that of speech. This transition from silence to speech is much discussed in most women writers of postmodern times. Whether named or unnamed, Kapur makes a conscious effort to portray these two types of women in most of her fiction. It is observed in Kapur's fiction that even though the younger women revolt at certain stages; yet, at times, they succumb to traditions. Kapur seems to suggest that women are always are caught in the web of tradition. For modern women who are educated and rational, it becomes difficult and hence there arises the conflicts. But unlike the women in Markandaya or Desai's fiction, these women in Kapur's texts do not just end with plain compromise but their reaction is much bolder and churns ways in a positive manner. Ranu Uniyal remarks:

> Contemporary women's fiction is a challenge to master narratives. At a manifest level it is an attempt to read life and rewrite the notion of subjectivity within the parameters of, difference. It focuses on differences that make a difference to women in a dominant masculine culture (56).

Out of all the novels written by Kapur, *Difficult Daughters* is a perfect example for the tensions and conflicts that arise in the individual psyche, between tradition and modernity. Shaleen Kumar comments on this clash:

> Manju Kapur's Difficult Daughters, her maiden novel published in 1998 is a perfect example of the clash of Tradition verses Modernity. The novel is written on the pre-independence background of Indian society that was facing long violent confrontation for freedom as well as the assault and onrush of modernity in form of new education or out loud voice of women (who, since middle ages, have been the victim of repressions and oppressions). Virmati, the epitome of modernity, has tried to break the trammels of traditions that have been binding her and obstructing her to cross tie-boundaries of customs and Sanskaras

> that have been prescribed by men and imposed by male-dominated society (11).

The image of women in the early fiction was one of mother, wife or daughter, someone who is self-sacrificing, enduring, meek and quiet woman. The conventional norms and stereotypical women figures underwent a change in the later phases of Indians writing in English. Growth of technology, communication, feminist movements and education has made people especially woman aware of their status in society and the need to uplift them. In recent authors like Manju kapur, we find woman throwing off the traditional baggage's that women had been carrying since ages. Women in literatures now emerge as assertive, self-assured, confident, educated, like to be financially independent and create an identity for themselves. Kapur's women characters yearn for freedom and space within the family threshold and the society outside. They strive for autonomy but at the same time, their familial duties as wife, mother or daughter are never at stake. Yet there is some conflict between traditional values and practices that they have seen and grown up with and the new emerging sense of modernity. The protagonists, therefore, struggle to find solace, assimilating the two worlds; the traditional and modern. Women novelists show serious concern towards the issues pertaining to woman. Still today, in the present era of post globalisation and post modernism, every day we hear about women being subjected various atrocities, social evils, humiliation, rape and sexual harassment. As N. Krishnaswami comments:

> In all traditions women have always been considered inferior and incapable of any serious thinking, irrespective of religion, country, race, the period in which they live, more or less the same perception and sex-stereotyping is seen in language and literature (4).

One of the factors that regulates in Indian society is the institution of marriage and this has been beautifully captured in Kapur's fiction. Every woman no matter what, at the end of the day is expected to get married. Societal pressure and familial traditions compel to meet the expected norms. Marriage in India becomes a family occasion and the concept of family and with it the relations become a major importance. Kasturi, mother of Virmati, feels, "it is the duty of every girl to get married." (*Difficult Daughters* 15) Astha's mother in *A Married Woman*, says to Astha,

> When you are married, our responsibilities will be over. Do you know the Shastras say if Parents die without getting their daughter married, they will be condemned to perpetual rebirth. (*A Married Woman* 01).

Nina's mother in *The Immigrant* has a similar preoccupation:

> The major topic of conversation in the last eight years had been Nina's marriage-who, whom, where, how? From where could fresh possibilities be unearthed on the eve of her thirtieth birthday? The lack of these, reflected in her mother's dull, mournful eyes, was what she was going home to (*The Immigrant* 03).

Nina's mother worries about her daughter who has turned thirty and yet is not married. For her, Nina's unfertilised eggs are not contributing to her womanhood. Nina realises "We are conditioned to think a woman's fulfilment lies in birth and motherhood, just as we are conditioned to feel failures if we don't marry" (233).

Marriage is also discussed in *Home* and *Custody* as well showing clearly the Indian mindset of preoccupation of marriage and related rituals. Marriage, thus, controls and governs Indian psyche and the society.

On the other hand, educated woman like Shakuntala Penji, cousin of Virmati in *Difficult Daughters* says:

> These people dont't really understand Viru, how much satisfaction there can be in leading your own life, in being independent. Here we are, fighting for the freedom of the nation, but woman are still supposed to marry, and nothing else (*Difficult Daughters* 17).

Alienation is one thing that most of Kapur's characters feel. Virmati feels alienated at her home when no one at home is able to understand her. Then, when she becomes the second wife of the professor, she feels lonely again, adjusting to a new environment.

In traditional Indian societies, men hold power within the household and also outside. The Professor's wife Ganga in *Difficult Daughters* acknowledges that men control their lives. She never questions him for anything. "His authority in the house meant that nobody openly questioned his statement" (84). Traditional women do not value education and it is considered a waste, as woman's role is confined to family. Kapur believes that tradition should be followed but not in blind way. This is reinforced through Harish, the Professor in *Difficult Daughters*.

> .... our education leads us to the question same of the value systems by which we live, that is not to say that we are destroying tradition. The tradition that refuses to entertain doubt, or remains impervious to new thoughts and ideas becomes a prison rather than a sustaining life force. Even the smallest one of us has a social function, but that function is not to follow blindly beliefs that may not be valid (102).

Shagun, the protagonist in *Custody* is bold enough to go against the patriarchal orders set for women. She wants a care free life and asserts her individuality by making a free choice. She is not bothered about what people or society would say about her act. She willingly gives way to her love found in Ashok Khanna, her husband's boss. Her mother is worried about this extra marital affair and determines "She had needed to ensure her daughter's safety before the fruit was snatched and a tender life ruined" (Kapur 38). Initially, Shagun is portrayed by the author as a traditional woman confined to wifely duties at home but when she meets her husband's boss, her life takes a different turn. She realises that she had not been happy with her life. She regrets "She had been brought up to marry, to be wife, mother and daughter-in-law. She had never questioned this destiny, it was the one pursued by everyone she knew" (Kapur 27). The tension between tradition and modernity is well represented through the psyche of Shagun who is torn between her duty towards family and personal aspirations. She desperately wants freedom and love which she finds in her lover's companionship. Yet her motherly feelings towards her kids shake her desire. But she takes a bold decision of perceiving her desires at the cost of losing her family. And at times she makes a thousand resolutions "be wife like, be good, docile, compliant but the mere sight of him sent these decisions out the window" (49-50). When Shagun is bothered about what her children will think of her, Ashok, her lover says: "By the time your children grow up the whole world will have changed. Certainly this benighted country. Things are moving so fast as it is" (84). He is aware of this dichotomy. "Traditional versus modern values, individual versus society" (84). Shagun and Ishita are two contrasting characters in the novel. Shagun aspires for individual freedom and happiness. For Ishita happiness lies in family and motherhood. One is portrayed as the modern and the other the traditional women. For each of them happiness differs. For these two women, the choices are different. Kapur perhaps hints that choices that we make govern our happiness and there are also certain things which leave no choice to shape our destiny.

4.3 Conflict between Emotion and Pragmatism

Virmati is torn between duty and desire. Her one side has feelings for her family members and the other side; she is unable to forget the professor with whom she is deeply in love. Love makes her blind and her heart rules over her mind. She falls for a man who is already married and has children. Virmati faces tremendous conflict with her mind which gives her rational thoughts and her heart which is full of love for Harish. Harish also loves her equally but he is unable to take any decision. His duty consciousness towards his wife and children makes him hesitant to marry Virmati. Although western educated, he is bound by tradition and societal values and hence cannot take any hasty step. It's only on Virmati's insistence that they both get married. Although Harish is western educated and has liberal views, yet he has to abide by his conscious self to his society.

The inner turmoil of being in-betweeness and the resultant conflicts becomes part of the narrative in *A Married Woman* and

Custody. Both Astha and Shagun are caught between the need for personal freedom and happiness and harsh realities of taking an unusual path. Astha enjoys her sexual intimacy with Pipeelika but her duty consciousness as a wife and mother makes her part from her sexual partner. Shagun too faces such a dilemma of being with family or her lover. But she dares and boldly takes the step of leading a life which will give her more happiness. Against all conflicting situations, she finally goes to meet her heart's desire.

Desire, passion and duty consciousness is the major tension that all of Kapur's protagonist face. These conflicts and tensions get manifested in the form of headaches, skin diseases and other health conditions.

4.4 Values and Ethics

Women in Indian society are so bound by family, society, rituals, tradition that they hardly find any space for themselves. They are so preoccupied and at times, even if they realise to become independent and search for meaning in their own life, they find it difficult to abandon all priorities that were so long taken care. Hence, there always arises conflict between individual freedom and happiness and the private world of women. Such conflicting status and the trauma of the mind is reflected through headaches which most of her central characters experience. Headache becomes like a metaphor indicating confusion, agony and helplessness. This dichotomy between familial ties and personal choice is skillfully narrated by Kapur through the headache episodes. Astha, Nisha, Virmati, Shagun and Nina, all suffer from headaches during their mid of life.

In *Custody,* Shagun is apprehensive with her relationship with Ashok. Shagun says to her lover Ashok, "How will they (children) like it when they grow up and realise their mother is a divorcee? (*Custody* 81).

For this Ashok replies:

> What is there to realise? This is why I hate this fucking place. This obsession with what others think. By the time your children

> grow up the whole world will have changed. Certainly this benighted country. Things are changing fast as it is. Ten years ago you couldn't get a coke, a pizza or a burger here. Things are moving fast as it is... Tradition vs. modern values, individual versus society. I just want to take you away from here. This narrow social set up is all you know-that's why you are afraid. But it will all be fine, fine... We only have one life to live and everybody wants to live it the best they can (*Custody* 81).

For Shagun, motherhood was holding her back and reminding of her motherly duties and thus making her hesitant to get away with Ashok. So was Astha, who couldn't move away with Pipeelika, just because of her children and her said responsibilities.

In Indian societies, when a woman is unable to bear children, she is rejected, looked down upon and is subject to various taunts. Ishita in *Custody* faces this. Her husband Suryakant, stopped even having any talks with her and last night "last night he moved to his parents' bedroom. She felt degraded, a non-person, certainly a non-woman. He was determined there should be nothing left between them" (*Custody* 69).

Shagun's motherly duties compel her not to be firm in her decision in leaving Raman where as Ishita's inability to become a mother becomes a misfortune for her. There is conflict between traditional values and modern ideas put forth by Ashok. For Sagun's mother "the house rests upon us women. In your children's happiness, lies your husband's happiness lies your own. Anything else is just temporary" (*Custody* 99). Ashok comments "The great Indian family, which rested on the sacrifices of its women" (*Custody* 99).

Manju Kapur lays emphasis on family. In one of her interview, she tells:

> I place a fair amount of emphasis on family because I look at the family as the nucleus of our life. This is where you have your children, where they develop values. And they eventually grow up and go out into the world with those values (www.hinduonnet.com).

In Jhumpa Lahari's fiction, marriage brings women to a new environment; they are dislocated in foreign land. But in Kapur's fiction, marriage becomes a boundary for women who intend to oscillate within its given framework in order to sustain family life and responsibilities. Alienation, frustration and loneliness make Anita Desai's women characters hysterical. This situation is shown in the form of series of headaches in Kapur's women characters. Astha for example, initially yearns for Hemant's love and attention but later she understands that what she requires is self-independence and a space of her own.

Every society has certain values and norms. Family, relationships, the bond between husband and wife, rituals and traditions are highly valued in Indian society. But these are also questioned and challenged due to modernization and change and also ensues conflicts. Off late, Indian English fiction is keen to explore the psychological and sociological strains in the social and individual life, trying to unite the past traditional values with the fast-emerging realities of modern life. Old orders are redefined and a kind of gradual metamorphosis and synthesis of the old and the new is observed in recent women writers. The crisis in the values of family and marriage are seen in the fiction of Kamala Markandaya, Ruth Prawer Jhabwala, Nayantara Sehgal, Anita desai, Bharati Mukherjee, Shashi Deshpande, Jhumpa lahiri and Manju Kapur.

Kapur shows that traditions and conventions are so deeply rooted in our Indian psyche that it is quite difficult to erase them. Astha's "MBA, foreign returned" (33) husband, craves for male child and his patriarchal attitude disturbs her. Harish in *Difficult Daughters* has negligent attitude towards his first wife Ganga who is an illiterate.

The conflicts between education, westernisation and that of traditional practices are much discussed in these novels. It is not only women but men also suffer under the so – called systems. In one of his letters to Virmati, Harish says:

> Education leads us to question some of the value system by which we live, that is not to say that we are destroying traditions.

> The tradition that refuses to entertain doubt, or remains impervious to new thoughts and ideas, becomes a poison rather than a sustaining life force. Even the smallest one of us has a social function, but that may not be value (102).

The author through Harish seems to hint that the traditional and modern values should be harmoniously balanced to keep human life comfortable. Blind practices should be reconsidered and our existing rigid practices must be modified and should undergo transition to meet modern requirements. New humanistic traditions should be incorporated for the betterment of human life.

Kapur seems to voice: sexuality and gender becomes a site of oppression, family becomes a site of oppression, traditions, customs give rise to oppression, and society becomes site of oppression. In all these sites, both the genders suffer but it is women who are larger victims.

Conflict between tradition and postmodernity, emotion and pragmatism, values and ethics, desire and duty, love and familial commitment are some of the author's prime concern.

4.5 Empowering Women and Thought Processes

One of the predominant concerns of Indian writers was concern for the girl child and woman's empowerment. Contemporary writer, Manju Kapur is one such writer. Being a professor and academician herself, she has poignantly crafted the value of women's education and made a critique of education from a feminine standpoint. A close reading of her fiction suggests the value and importance of education in every woman's life, as pointed out in a delicate manner. Kapur voices the fact that autonomy and economic independence can be achieved through education.

Difficult Daughters is a story narrated by the protagonist Virmati's daughter Ida. Both Virmati and Ida are 'difficult' as they rebel against the traditional roles expected from them. The story is set against the backdrop of India's freedom struggle, its attainment and partition thereafter. The turmoil and pain that Virmati undergoes is aptly suggested through the freedom struggle of the country to free away from oppression. The novel skillfully unfolds with multiple subjects like self-affirmation, man-woman relationship, family feuds and above all mother-daughter relationship. From an early age, Virmati starts looking after her young siblings for whom she is 'second mother' and the domestic chores without any recognition and love from her mother. This lack of love and longing to gain attention gradually makes her fall in love with a married professor which the family is totally against. Motivated by the idea of true love, self-realisation and independence, Virmati undergoes a series of humiliations which eventually makes her to be firmer in her decisions. The professor is caught between his wife and the lover who could fulfill his intellectual needs. As no solution creeps in, Virmati decides to go for higher studies. She understands that education could give her enlightenment and freedom. Even the professor's wife realises that "It is good the girls of today know so much." The value of education and the importance it carries in a person's life is clearly indicated. The professor working in a college symbolises higher education. But since his wife is uneducated, he abandons her. His wife is submissive as she has no knowledge of the outer world. Every uneducated woman would feel that ignorance, lack of freedom and oppression suffered is due to lack of education. Kapur hints that women can be emancipated through education. Education makes us to think rationally, makes one realise and this, in turn, paves way for self-independence. Virmati is educated but she goes for higher education to free from everyday problems and make some life for her own. But she wants a name for the relationship she has and finally the professor agrees to marry her and she becomes his second wife. The value of education is also voiced through Virmati's friend Swarnalata. Virmati's problems do end not there and there comes another set of problems for her – her life and adjustment in her married household as a second wife. Life continues for her with its odds and ends, but Kapur has subtly brought out the idea of liberation through education. The theme of alienation, self-assertion and identity is interwoven skillfully through the idea of educating oneself. In most of Kapur's novels, we have at least one character who works as a principal/ professor or teacher in educational institutions. The portrayal of institutions of higher education and the central characters moving for higher education is noteworthy. Not all Indian English women writers have been careful to portray this aspect. Hence, we see this strong message in a very subtle way. In *A Married Woman*, the central character Astha has everything that a woman could ask for, but there is some gap between the husband and the wife. Astha, just after marriage became a school teacher. She yearned for some time from her husband but he was "a criminal, destroying her anticipation, ruining her happiness" (50). Gradually Astha turns to writing poetry and this alleviates the heaviness within her. But remarks from Hemant, her husband, make her leave writing and switch to sketching and drawing. Soon, she enters into a lesbian relationship with Aijaz's wife Pipeelika after Aijaz's death. Though Astha and Pipeelika are into this relationship, yet they know how futile it is. Astha cannot leave her family and Pipeelika can't expect much from her. Towards the end of the novel, we find Pipeelika leaving for the USA to do her Ph. D as suggested by her brother who sponsors her. Manju Kapur also shows that life is a labyrinth. Whatever happens with us, we finally return to the conventional set up. Both Virmati and her daughter Ida accept this and try to fit themselves into it. Astha too knows that whatever happened outside her married life is only temporary and she is bound to go back to her earlier life.

Women's empowerment, as Kapur points out in her fiction, can be defined in terms of achieving power in order to take part in decision making, designing their lives, influencing the social and political process. Formal Education need not necessarily be a tool to emancipate women. Women learning to defy themselves and making their own identity are empowered. Though education cannot bring complete emancipation, it has an immense effect on the lives of women. According to the feminists' view, education has to generate awareness and make women ask questions about their condition in order to move towards empowerment.

Manju Kapur's protagonists are women trying to maintain a balance all the time. Their everyday struggles have made them strong and they struggle to set themselves free from the shackles of tradition and various prejudices. All of Kapur's female protagonists are well educated but again they are seen heading for higher education. In Kapur's fiction, we also find female characters probing into literature and reading books to seek solace and companionship. *Difficult Daughters* explores the possibilities of change in attitude through exposure to literature. *The Immigrant* is another book where these aspects are exposed in a diaspora set up. Nina, in *The Immigrant* works as a lecturer in a college. She is married to Ananda, a dentist settled in Canada. The novel is a story about the adjustments that Indian expatriates have to make when settled abroad. The journey of Nina is a journey from a traditional upbringing to freedom and liberation as defined in a foreign land. Nina's life with Ananda is not a satisfactory one. Soon, she discovers that her husband has sexual dysfunctions and hence avoids her. He goes for a treatment without her knowledge and later experiments his sexual pangs with white women. Nina pursues her studies in library science and takes a career in a library. She seeks professional identity as a student of library science. Nina finds some kind of fulfillment by associating with a group of women. There are literary reference points to DH Lawrence, E.M Foster as Nina is a voracious reader. Her association with Sue's La Leche League and Beth's support group expose her to the western concepts of liberation, freedom, rebellion, courage, integrity and individual woman self. She reads for the first time, beyond authors like Lawrence, *The Second Sex* and *The Female Eunuch*. Towards the end, we find Nina heading out for a job interview at the University of New Brunswick, uncertain if she will return to her Halifax life or not. It feels, though, as if she is now ready to take control of her own destiny – 'heading towards fresh territories, a different set of circumstances... When one was reinventing oneself, anywhere could be home' (*The Immigrant* 334). The reader may, nonetheless, fairly ask what is that Nina is reinventing herself as.

One of the key features of Kapur's writings is her constant preoccupation of women's issues. She particularly focuses on women's constant negotiation with her private and public life. Manju Kapur's *Home* is a story about Indian joint family; Manju Kapur weaves universal truths about the complexities of extended families and the pull of tradition against modernity. The patriarch of the family is Banwari Lal, a cloth merchant who lives with his family in Karol Bagh, New Delhi. The Banwari Lal family belongs to a class whose skills have been honed over generations to ensure prosperity in market place. From an early age, children are trained to maintain the foundation on which their homes rested. Banwari Lal is believer of older ways. Men work out of home and women within. His two sons unquestioningly follow their father in business and in life but their wives do not. Contemporary women writers like Kapur, through their texts, question the age-old traditions and patriarchal system and show signs of resistance to them. They re-represent women in their postmodern narratives. Hence there are strong and bold women characters. They question the idea of 'being an ideal woman'. She critiques the patriarchal power structure of Hindu society through the characters. She deconstructs the notions of gender, equality and identity through the narrative. She has also pointed that however educated and forward notions, yet in Indian society, still the longing for a male child is prevalent. In *Home*, after Sona gives birth to a male child, the mother-in-law declared, "Now I can die in peace" (*Home* 41). Nisha who is the protagonist has some difficult phases of childhood and adolescence. College education makes her life stable and independent. Later, Nisha strives to establish her individuality and becomes an entrepreneur. She starts her own business of garment stitching. After making her presence felt in primarily a male dominated profession; she had to fall in the same trap of matrimony ascribed by the patriarchy. But she was ready for the same i.e. to shoulder responsibility not only of husband and children but beyond that. Nisha is a confident, self-reliant, bold and determined person, who defies patriarchal notions. She establishes her own boutique and names her products 'Nisha creations'. Once economically emancipated, she throws social codes to the wind and proves herself to be a responsible working businesswoman. Thus, we learn that education boosted self-confidence and economic independence and thereby creating an identity for oneself.

After the introduction of western education, significantly with the advent of colonialism in India under the British Empire, reformist movements, promotion of women's institutions, the freedom movement and so on, life had begun to change once more. In post-Independence India, where education of women had already commenced, the New Woman also had begun to emerge. Education had inculcated a sense of individuality amongst women and had aroused an interest in their human rights. It was then that the feminist trend in Indian literature had appeared on the horizon and women came into conflict with the double standards of social law through ages and the conventional moral code. Feminist ideology in Indian literature, which had come into India precisely from the west and the women`s liberation movement is not widely spread into India, as fighting for human rights of women has been misinterpreted as movement against Indian womanhood. In post-Independent India, the educated New Woman with economic independence and a search for identity is clearly depicted in fiction.

Good education consists of a balance between passion and pragmatism, which are opposing forces. In today's fast-paced world, the researcher feels that there is a distortion of importance and perception in this balance. Therefore, the need arises to focus on a writer like Manju Kapur who foregrounds women who come to a cross junction in life where they wonder which way they should go. The texts, which bear testimony to characters who step in and step out due to their sex impulses and their final decision to be pragmatic through a compromise, form the essence of the study.

Resistance to patriarchy starts with Virmati's insistence on education and refusal for marriage. She believes: "One of the benefits of education is that it teaches us to think for ourselves" (*Difficult Daughters* 102). She wants to live an intellectual life of mind, but the society in the guise of her parents reminds her that a woman is no more than a body and the patriarchal society permits no alternative to marriage and holds in pity and contempt those who attempt to thwart it. Virmati resists this patriarchy. She is brought up in an Arya Samaj house and is sent to a Samaj school and college. The Arya Samaj encourages women's education and discourages child marriages and conversion to Christianity.

Kapur has a straight forward approach in her novels. She gives us real characters and real examples from the society. It is important to suggest that Kapur's novels refuse to supply any obvious, specific and direct viewpoints. Kapur believes in 'showing' instead of 'telling'. She would rather problematise than provide solutions. Her descriptive mode of narration combined with an objective outlook and open endings place her in the postmodern domain. Kapur does not point that education will eradicate all problems. In fact, Kapur's major women characters are well educated. She suggests that education will make us more rational and enable us to think more independently to solve our problems. Although already educated, some of the characters are shown to pursue higher studies. Perhaps reading good books and keeping oneself professionally busy either in work or studies would make us more preoccupied and less worried. This is what some Kapur's characters tend to realise.

Kapur's most recent novel *Custody* (2011) is a story about infidelity and infertility resulting in marital discord which has tremendous impact on the lives of the children. It is also the tale of children's custody and the Indian legal system. The plot of *Custody* is set in the backdrop of urban upper middle class family of Delhi. Kapur explores the hollowness of modern life. The story revolves around the couple Raman and Shagun, along with charismatic Ashok Khanna, who is Raman's boss; and Ishita, a childless divorcee. Kapur uses the institution of marriage, in this novel, to present the story of four adults and two children. A sequence of dispute follows along with arguments, heated discussions, exposing the evil side of divorce. Kapur through Ishita's life exposes the shallowness of marital life where a woman is stigmatised because of her infertility and the fact that she can't carry forward the family name. Ishita was happy after marriage but when she could not bear him a child, all her miseries started. Her husband and mother in law threw her out of the house. When she was divorced, her parents were her support. To overcome her sadness, she started working as a social worker and teaching the under privileged. Like in most Kapur's novel, the teaching profession enters here as well. This could be because Kapur herself is first a teacher and academician. Hence, the role of education, the teaching profession becomes some of Kapur's habitual references.

Further, Kapur's novels clearly state the conviction that higher education and economic independence support women to take independent decisions. Her novels also state that the lens of education and economic independence helps to mitigate the threats of violence which women have to face in various relationships. This aspect is also commented on by several other critics also. Manju Kapur's first novel *Difficult Daughters* narrates the story of Virmati, the protagonist whose struggles for liberation is supported by her education. She is very much influenced by her cousin Shakuntala, who is depicted as a qualified woman, a woman of substance, who holds the view that "here we are, fighting for the freedom of the nation, but women are still supposed to marry, and nothing else" (DD 17). Shakuntala's portrayal narrates how in a patriarchal society, a woman is respected and considered to be honorable only if she is limited to her roles of a wife and mother. Her family's aggressive refusal to allow her to study further leads Virmati to Harish Chandra, a professor from England who not only expresses his vision towards women's education but also encourages Virmati for further study. Professor Harish Chandra becomes a spokesperson for Kapur when he says:

> For him, too, studies are very important. It showed he really cared for women's education ...who is responsible for this state of affairs? Society, which deems that their sons should be educated, but not their daughters. Once she had gained a proper education, she would be on her way to becoming one of the finest flowers of Hindu womanhood (*Difficult Daughters* 103).

Education and the resulting financial independence is what Kapur is aiming at to project. Education should be sort for shaping one's individual make up not for the sake of being a potential candidate and enhancing opportunities in the marriage market. Though Virmati's mother accuses her even after her education and career growth for ruining family honour, it is her father who remains supportive and sends her for higher education. In *Married Woman*, Astha's father is liberated and believes that his daughter must study to expand her mental horizon. He "believes in the new. He feels that his daughter's future lay in her own hands, and these hands were to be strengthened by the number of books that passed through them" (*A Married Woman* 2).

Her father, a bureaucrat, does not want his daughter to be like himself—disssatisfied and wasted. He preaches her to work hard to create her own opportunities, "You are so much potential, you draw, you paint, you read, you have a way with words, you do well academically, the math's is a little weak, but never mind, you must sit for the competitive exams. With a good job comes independence" Kapur has shown her male characters supporting female education for independence. But at the same time she has pointed that our patriarchal society wants women to be married and to stay in husband's house as that alone brings self-respect and dignity for a woman. So, there is a conflict perhaps between education and marriage, women's free will and societal expectations. Sometimes, women are allowed to continue studies till a suitable match is found. This happens with Nisha in *Home.* She is given higher education as the family is not able to find a 'manglik' match for her. Even then, she is told not to take it seriously, "Higher studies were just a time pass, it was not as though she was going to use her education. Working was out of the question, and marriage was around the corner" (*Home* 141). Kapur voices the need for self-independence through Nisha who says: "I want to study fashion designing. Lots of girls do it.... I have seen girls working in shops. Why should it be only Ajay, Vijay and Raju? There must be something I too can do" (*Home* 226-267) In *Custody*, Mrs Hingorani says: "It will get you a job with more income, and that spells respect and independence" (*Custody* 178). Ishita decides to pursue MA in Social Work from the Institute of Social Welfare in Bombay.

Manju Kapur has very clearly pointed that women's education makes them to self-realise and be more independent. Reading through the texts, we understand how women are conditioned to accept marriage and familial responsibilities as their sole purpose of life and getting education is a means to find a potential suitor in the marriage market. Not only this, we are also allowed to think about how some careers are specifically thought to be performed only by men; gender permeating through education and learning as well. Through subtle narration, Kapur has skillfully not only emphasised the value and role of education in women's lives but at the same time made a critique of education itself by questioning the very notion of education and career based on gender in a patriarchal society.

The significance of education in man-woman relationship can be observed from Harish's words:

> We have nothing in common. I once wanted to share my interests with my wife, felt her pain at my estrangement from her.... Who is responsible for this state of affairs? Society which deems that their sons should be educated, but not their daughters (*Difficult Daughters* 95).

The significance of education regarding women's independence is realised even today. It is education that enables women to realise the nature of their subjugation, marginalisation and suppression and helps find effective ways to check it and acquire a self-dependent, autonomous self. The following words bring out the significance of education for woman's freedom.

> Now the new education has awakened her real self. As a result of this she has started thinking of independent and self-reliant life. And in order to translate this thinking into reality, she has started fighting against her own timid self as well as man's protectoral shell (Barche1995: 130).

Thus, Kapur's message is loud and clear that "society would be better off if its females were effective and capable" (*Difficult Daughters* 163).

From an analysis of the conflicts reflected in Kapur's works, it can be concluded that the strains in human relations, emotional imbalances, failure to accept reality, a feeling of low self-esteem and so on are responsible for various conflicts. This is to say that the conflicts are mind, body and environment driven.

4.6. Language and Narrative Art

Narrative strategy is the use of certain narrative techniques and practices by the author to convey what they want to the audience. In simple terms, it can be said as the method of conveying. In fictions, the author adopts various methods and techniques to reveal the story. The traditional linear method of storytelling with a beginning, middle and end with realistic approach gave way for more explorative forms in the modern and postmodern period. The stream of consciousness technique which enables the writer to delineate the running thoughts of the characters and the workings of their mindscape is explicitly found in the writings of modern period. In postmodern writings, especially in fictions we find numerous examples that suggest how the art of narration manifests itself in different forms. This form of experimentation is observed in Indian Writing in English as well. Recasting and reinterpreting myths and legends become a prevalent practice among writers in order to make their works locally situated rather than universally relevant. Chronologically ordered narration is replaced by fragmented and non-linear presentation. The postmodern tendency of abandoning omniscient authorship becomes visible in the novels of the period. The omnipresent narrator who pretends to know everything and who makes judgment upon characters gives way to polyphonic or multi-voiced narratives. Different narrative techniques are subtly interwoven into the texture and structure in Indian English fiction. Gita Hariharan and Shashi Deshpande make ample use of legends and myths of India to unfold the story. These myths, legends and folk narratives become the part of main stream narrative which are retold by the characters in a different way to suit the author's intention. Indian epics, the *Puranas* and *Ithihasas* like the *Mahabharata,* the *Ramayana, the Panchathantra* stories, the *Jataka* tales, the *Bhagavad Gita* or the *Gitopadesham,* the *Upanishads* provide a rich platform for exploration for Indian writers. Postcolonial writers show their resistance to the imperial centre and reject the traditional methods of narrations followed by the novelists of canonical literature. Thus, instead of mimicking the West, Indian writers started trying to rejuvenate their own cultural heritage and traditional practices of writing. The ultimate intention of these writers is to create an identity for themselves, which, they feared were lost in the colonial power structure. Usage of multiple voices of multiple narratives is clearly seen in Amitav Ghose, Gita Hariharan and many others. The different techniques adopted are: fragmented way of storytelling, usage of story within the story, using unreliable narrator, magic realism and sub stories find place in postmodern writings. If Salman Rushdie and Gita Hariharan choose to use magic realism, Gita Mehta's *A River Sutra* draws our attention to the multiple stories embedded within the main plot. India's history also becomes a framework on which the major plot works. History is relooked and considered for examination. Contemporary writers make ample use of history to revaluate and reconsider it for the story to unfold. They depict how the historical events affected the lives of the individuals. They bring to light the untold stories and subjects. They strongly believe that since the history of postcolonial territories was, until recently, largely a narrative constructed by the colonisers, its fictions and languages in which they are written operate as a means of cultural control. They resort to history with the purpose of finding its relevance to contemporary issues, to caricature the present personalities, to allegorise, to record the unrecorded, to give voice to the subaltern, to subvert it, to question the hegemony, to unfold the constructedness of many ideas, concepts and truths, to interrogate the concept of nation and finally to present their point of view through it. Salman Rushdie's *Midnight's Children*, Shashi Tharoor's *The Great Indian Novel* and Amitav Ghosh's *The Calcutta Chromosome* are good examples for this.

Globalisation is presented through shifting locales and characters that become global. This is done to convey the idea that this is the order of the day in the globalised situation and to show the resistance to the idea of unity of place. So, the actions in the novels of many novelists take place in different places of the world. For instance, Vikram Seth sets the scene of his *The Golden Gate* in the U.S.A. and *An Equal music* in European countries. In Amitav Ghosh's *The Circle of Reasons* and *The Glass Palace*, the actions take place in India, the U. S.A., Burma and Egypt. Some of the major narrative devices the writers of this period employ are non-linear plots, multiple narration, flash back and flash forward, anti-heroes and heroines, more about common men, magic realism, intertexuality, mixed genres, story within story, chutnification of words and so on. A good usage of flashback technique is observed in Arundhati Roy's *The God of Small things*. In Amitav Ghosh's *The Hungry Tide*, the story naturally unfolds through the perspective of different characters-cum-narrators. An unnamed fictional narrator functions like a commentator and interconnects the missing links in the novel. Another striking characteristic of postmodern Indian fiction is the deliberate use of indianised English words. Experimentation with language is clearly noticed. Coining of words, usage of regional words and phrases, alliteration, code mixing and code switching are spread over the narrative art. In their seminal work *The Empire Writes Back*, Ashcroft et al., assert that postcolonial writers employ the highly developed strategy of code-switching and vernacular transcription which achieves the dual result of abrogating the Standard English and appropriating an English as a culturally significant discourse (Ashcroft et al., 1989: 45). Indian writers try to evolve flexible English that would convey the nuances of Indian life. The Indian English novelists, by using various linguistic and stylistic devices, have succeeded in infusing the rhythm of Indian languages into English and in conveying the Indian sensibility. Meenakshi Mukherjee states that the style is not integral to the author's point of view but something added to the material like "icing on the cake or embroidery on a sari". Further she writes: "No amount of experimentation with style, no amount of conscious innovations will succeed in fiction unless it has inevitability in the context of the particular theme the novel deals with" (63).

In the context of art, narration and style, Manju Kapur's oeuvre undoubtedly makes the reader to observe the way the story gets unfolded along with the rendering of the plot. An artist must possess the art of narration along with the theme; Kapur makes a good impact on her readers through the art of narration. Kapur, uses the realistic mode of approach in her novels. She talks about reality, the roots of Indian psyche, family-centred life, generation gap and all real-life situations that she sees around. Her descriptions are detailed but she does not give much detailed description about landscape or the place. But ample words are used to describe a character or situation. Kapur believes in 'showing' rather than 'telling'. She would rather problematise than provide solutions. Much in the manner of R. K. Narayan, she abstains from passing judgements. Her descriptive mode of narration combined with an air of detachment and open endings place her in the postmodern domain. It is observed that few postmodern writers like Kapur refrained from magic realism and chose to revive the social realism and traditional linear narrative technique that was quite popular at the initial stages of fictional writings. Some of the striking narrative strategies adopted by Kapur in her novels are: use of history, role of memory, flashback technique, abundant use of food imagery, use of sensual images, using letters and diary form, multiple perspectives, shift of locales, code switching and code mixing. Above all, Kapur's fictions are hallmark of social realism with a postmodern twist.

In *Difficult Daughters*, Virmati's story is told from a present day perspective by Ida, her only daughter, who ventures to investigate and reconstruct her late mother's life story out of the folds of past. The novel is set against the backdrop of independence movement of the 1940s and the subsequent trauma of partition. The story at the onset opens with a present day situation where we find the funeral of Virmati and Ida declaring that "the one thing I had wanted was not to be like my mother". From here, the story takes a backward turn and events are narrated through a flash back technique. But the narrative does not unfold in a systematic linear fashion but it is fragmented. Different events and incidents are pieced together and Ida based on her collective experience and gatherings, unfolds the story to us. We learn about Virmati through this piecing together of memories by various characters, told to the reader by Ida. Thus, as a postmodern text, the fiction relies on memory, the past and has fragmented narration and multiple perspectives. It is to be noted that the other novels of Kapur do not employ the fragmented way of narration but has linear narrative structure. One characteristic feature of postmodern texts is the reliance on history. Manju Kapur chooses to use this technique as well. India's past, its struggle for independence and its final attainment and the later consequences go parallel as the main stream story unfolds. History acts as a backdrop and it complements the struggles and anguishes portrayed in the life of main characters. Kapur beautifully lays a woman's struggle for personal freedom, its attainment and the aftermath by interweaving the two manifestations – woman's struggle for independence in a tradition bound patriarchal framework and country's struggle for independence from the colonial clutches. This use of history to act as a platform appears in other novels of Kapur as well. In *A Married Woman,* the backdrop is the sensitive issue of Ram Janma – Babri masjid issue which is highlighted. Kapur, amply makes her female characters participate in freedom struggle. She showcases how women also came out of their domestic lives and participated in political scenario. This aspect we notice in both these novels. In *A Married Woman*, the highly disputed and controversial topic of Ram Janma – Babri masjid issue goes parallel with another controversial issue i.e. lesbianism. The central character Astha, inspite of having a 'complete family' finds herself completely unsatisfied with her marital life. She longs for love and companion and this she seeks through a relation with another woman by name Pipeelika. There is a mention of Rajiv Gandhi's assassination by a suicide bomber in Tamil Nadu. Accordingly, two sensitive and much debated issues are revealed through this story. In *The Immigrant*, the story unfolds in a period which is recent but not contemporary, the 1970s of Indira Gandhi's Emergency. Although the main concern is migration and its aftermath, history too has its role in the novel.

Thus, history and woman's personal freedom and choice and their limitations are interwoven in each of these novels to suit the themes.

One particular observance in Kapur's fictions is the use of Letters and the Diary form. In *Difficult Daughters,* there is exchange of letters between Virmati and Professor Harish. We get to know about their relationship, love and longing and anguish through these letters. Several pages of the book are taken over in the form of letters. Precise mention of dates, day and year gives a realistic touch and relates to events. There are also some poetic verses and a discussion on what the verses convey. In *A Married Woman,* the diary form is used. The reader gets to learn the story from the jottings on the diary. Astha's diary reveals different aspects of her life. Astha writes poetry and when her husband reads it aloud, we actually read the verses. We also get to read some actual letters written by Astha's mother to her. Another female character Pipeelika, has letters coming from her mother who consoles her with the tragedy of losing the husband. The letter reflects the agony and Pipeelika's marital life. Instead of having an omniscient narrator, there are these letters in Kapur's fiction which are nothing but devices to point out the inner working of the mind of the characters. In *The Immigrant* too, we witness exchange of letters between Ananda and Nina. Letters exchanged between mother and daughter or between lovers gives us insight about these characters. These devices authenticate what is being narrated. Astha's diary with dates and details gives a realistic touch. The diary form not only narrates the incidents but supports the realistic approach which Kapur has consciously chosen. Hence, as a narrative device, Kapur has used the letter and the diary form skillfully.

One thing particularly striking with Kapur's fiction is the ample use of sensory images, especially, the food imagery. Kapur's fictions are abundant with food imagery. She beautifully uses food as an image and metaphor to suggest complex ideas and inner tribulations. Food and eating symbolise cultural issues of acceptance, resistance, and preservation of culture, as well as symbols of memory, emotions, narrative history, relationships, power, and consumption. Food metaphors, therein, reflect directly on the Indian cultural identity as one of political and social fragmentation, postcolonial hybridity, patriarchal oppression, and repressed sexual desire. Food becomes fundamental to a culture. At the very literal level, food related images in literature, particularly when used with rich details and descriptions, appeal to the senses of the reader, enhancing the realism of the work. They provide sensory images readers can relate to – especially sights, smells, and tastes that may be familiar to readers. In fiction, the usage of food is more than just a literary detail that provides readers with a realistic visual image. Food imagery helps readers to understand their characters' true identities, because in many ways, food defines people and cultures. Food and eating practices are essentially ways of defining a culture's ethnic identity, reflecting on those persons' identities within the culture. Food not only reflects and expresses personal identity in life and in literature; it also mirrors cultural identity and can create boundaries and differences between cultures. Food, therefore, becomes a cultural signifier. India has a diversified culture. India is a nation of many ethnic groups and cultures. Thus, one food item may not represent all the cultures in India. Food speaks of ethnic origin. Anita Desai's *Fasting Feasting*, Jhumpa Lahiri's *The Namesake* and Manju Kapur's fictions are abundant with food imageries. Using food images are particular with these novelists. Not all Indian writers choose to use them lavishly.

In *The Immigrant*, as the protagonist Nina more and more ceases to identify with India, the lexical Indianisms become thin. At the initial level, the pages are filled with Indian food lexicals. "turmeric, yellow turning brown as it bubbled in hot oil, red chillies that crackled as they roasted, onions and garlic that turned pink then brown, releasing sweet sharp smells, tomatoes that became soupy as they were swished around, cumin and coriander that gave out pungent flavours, these smells and imagined sights travelled across the world from north India to eastern Canada to kick her sharply in the stomach" (220). The list of vegetarian lexicals gradually gives way to non-vegetarian and western food items. She breaks her own image of being a devout traditional Hindu wife by stepping aside customs she practiced and embraced western lifestyle. She leaves her vegetarianism and starts to eat flesh. Though she knew it was not for convenience that she had decided to switch over but due to a sense of fragmentation and distress. That weekend Nina tasted everything one by one. "Red Meat. Flesh. Mammals. Cow. Cows that looked into your eyes-cows that her mother worshipped on fixed days of the Hindu calendar. She could have graduated to chicken from fish, but Nina did not want the dishonesty involved in these slow, cautious steps" (267). And Ananda looked over with relief promising himself that "he would have her eating Sirloin steak and loving it" and "from now on, there wouldn't be the trouble of always cooking dal for her, of making sure there was enough salad and veggies" (267). This scene shows transition and adoption of a different food culture, comfort and ease and also agony and expression of suppressed anger.

Foods like pickles are also abundant in the fictions. Pickles denote preservation and, in the novels, they could imply preservation of culture and tradition. In *Difficult Daughters,* the women of the house are engrossed in making pakoras. "Ah, pumpkin, potato, onion, and green chilli pakoras! Sweet, salty and sharp, with the sourness of chutney slathered on their golden crisp shells. But now what was the use of anything?" (68) says Virmati. This food image also suggests the sweet love life of Virmati with the professor and at the same time indicates the sourness which she is going to encounter. The repetitive use of food images and women's constinent absorbtion in processing and preparation of food is indicative of women's 'naturalised' gender performances and conditioning of thoughts that is set to perform based on gender. The spatial zones of kitchen and routine culinary related works suggest how the female gender is assigned to play its roles unquestionably. Virmati, Nina and Shagun question such gendered roles and stereotypes.

Post 1980, Indian English writers showed resistance to dominant colonial English language and used English as it is used in Indian context for creative expressions. Regional idioms and phrases, abundant use of regional words, code switching and code mixing were casually used. This indianisation of the English language gave Indian writing in English a distinct identity and flavour. Postmodern and post-colonial writers showed resistance to imperial power structures through creative expressions with experimentation with language, style and technique. In this aspect, contemporary writer Manju Kapur is no exception. Lot of Hindi and Punjabi words are used in the exchange of conversations between the characters. Where words from the vernacular are concerned, the novel abounds with such borrowings. They are from different languages: Hindi primarily, but also Punjabi as well. Hindi words like *are*, *hoon, chachi, behn* and expressions such as *hai re, bap re* are sprinked across the texts. The words may be categorised under several lexical fields, such as names of Gods, other Hindi and Urdu words, Indianisms, Indian words and expressions and translations of Indian expressions. The usage of indianised English is twofold. One, it gives a realistic approach to her novels making her characters like real life and blood characters talking to one another. The other is to promote a sense of appeal to readers. Usage of Indian words enables readers to attach themselves with the characters and the story line. Regional touch gives readers to attach themselves with characters, arouse interest and curiosity to follow the story. The indianisation of the language is thus a powerful medium of creating a link with the reader. Kapur candidly says that as a published author she wants to reach as many people as possible. Thus, the use of vernacular words not only sets realism but also connects readers to it.

Intertextuality, referring to other texts within the narrative is also being deployed at various stages of narration. For example, Virmati's situation at the hands of fate is described by bringing references to Lady Macbeth. The narrative describes:

> Eventually her tears stopped, and she lay drained and corpse-like...... Like Lady Macbeth, she had murdered sleep. How Harish's face had glowed as he murmured, tasted...... Given all that, she might as well wander around like Lady Macbeth. (*Difficult Daughters* 162).

To conclude, one can clearly see how Kapur manipulated different narrative techniques to inter weave her themes and the story line. A blend of modern and postmodern narrative structure cleverly finds place in Kapur's fictions.

5

Conclusion

This chapter summarises all the essential points discussed in the previous chapters. It is understood that in the fiction of male writers, the women characters usually had a secondary place. There were writers who chose women protagonists, but their portrayal of them was too romanticised. They were far from real life characters. Women were portrayed as enduring wife or sacrificing mother. Motherhood and wifely duties were glorified. The archetypal images of Sita and Draupadi helped to support the view that endurance, compromise and submissiveness are virtues associated with woman. Women's entry into the main stream literature paved way for shattering of such images. Towards the age of modernism, there was a transition from the traditional portrayal of women as silent sufferers to women who voiced their opinions and asserted their rights. From silence to speech and self-discovery is apparent. With the advent of woman's writing, postcolonial and feminist discourse in the postmodern era, these conventional ideas underwent a sea change. Writers like Gita Hariharan have reinterpreted myths and folk narratives and deconstructed the traditional ideas centering on the images. Her women characters question the existing system, breaking new grounds for growth and opportunities. Many women writers be it in English or their regional language have used literature as a medium for social activism and change for betterment of society and refining our thoughts. Mahasweta Devi has worked on similar grounds, voicing through literature her concerns for the marginalised and oppressed groups. Literature, thus, becomes a powerful medium for social consciousness. In this respect, contemporary author Manju Kapur has left no stone unturned to use her creative expressions to question, challenge and deconstruct issues that deeply embody the Indian psyche and arouse consciousness that awaken and leave scope for better society.

This book has attempted to analyse the works of Manju Kapur in the background of the elaborated discussion and analysis. An in-depth reading of Manju Kapur's novels clearly points out that the author, no doubt, is a social chronicler of the modern Indian society. Her novels are narrative responses to patriarchal hegemony. Elaine Showalter in 1977 pointed three major literary phases: a phase of imitation, phase of protest, a phase of self-discovery, resistance and search for meaningful existence. Kapur's fiction falls under the last phase. Her liberal, bold and frank expression of sex and sexuality distinguishes her postmodern sensibilities. She has vividly portrayed the Indian human psyche and the lives of middle class families and the world that centers women. In one of the interviews, she herself has stated that being a woman, it is easy for her to depict and relate to the women's world and therefore her text unconsciously covers the feminine world. But nevertheless, she cannot be labeled altogether as a feminist writer as she works on a larger platform. Her works show the problems faced by the educated middle class women and their negotiation with life to make things comfortable. She has shown her concern for not only the suffering women but also the ordeals faced by men and children at different walks of life. Her fiction is open ended, almost take the linear narrative form and focus on human relationships, family, passion and desire, values and the human predicament. The crux of her works incorporates serious gender concerns, issues of identity and the dichotomy between tradition and modernity. The upbringing of a female child, child sexual harassment, gender discrimination, the binary opposition of male/female, gender as social constructs and the lives of modern educated women who struggle between traditional values and modern ideologies are well portrayed.

> Post modernism constitutes the expressing of a contextual discourse that problematises other discourses and thus enables us to critically examine the givens of other discourses. It exists thus as an alternative discourse to prevent a hegemonic domination of any one discourse (Salat 36).

Being a postmodern writer, Kapur, through her fiction problematises certain issues. Post modernism advocates multiplicity, pluralism, and open endedness. Kapur's novels portray the plurality of female experiences and how each woman adopts different strategies for self-assertion and constructive growth. In each of her texts, we encounter women of different nature and aspiration. Contrasting women are shown in order to understand the issue better. Kapur juxtaposes the conventional women and the revolting women in her fiction. Virmati, Astha, Nina, Nisha, Ishita are all initially portrayed as the conventional types who confine themselves to the roles of mothers, daughters and wives, but gradually they realise their needs, revolt in order to have space for themselves and become assertive enough to voice their opinions. This transition is clearly shown in Kapur's women characters.

This chapter gives a brief summary of the major concerns raised by the Manju Kapur. First, her works concentrate on the gender aspect. Gender exerts enormous impact on our lives from the time of our birth, and we act out its cultural and social aspects at crucial moments of our lives: from birth to death. Gender is embedded so thoroughly in our institutions, our actions, our beliefs, and our desires, that it appears to us to be completely natural. Gender, apart from biological discrimination, is a social and cultural construction of masculinities and femininities. Gender operates within the patriarchal power structure. Manju Kapur in her fiction has neatly addressed some gender stereotyping prevalent in Indian society which are nothing but arbitrary practices and therefore has no rational justification. Kapur's fiction shows how gender is nothing but socially constructed processes and how women and men are bound by this gender consciousness. Kapur's women protagonist revolt and resist patriarchal power structures to challenge male/female binary oppositions that operate within the family and also in the social domain.

Kapur represents her characters through the mode of bildungsroman. This strategy gives us the knowledge of one's upbringing and the processes that shaped one's behaviour and thinking. As soon as a baby is born, it is catagorised as male or female. Immediately everyone around speaks and expects to behave accordingly. Gender consciousness is deeply rooted in the psyche that most often it is thought natural and correct. Each of the female protagonists of Kapur is conscious of their gender roles. A girl child is expected to share the domestic works of her mother and also nurse her siblings. This happens in case of Virmati in *Difficult Daughters*. She becomes the second mother for her siblings at home and everyone expects to perform these tasks. No one seems to care about Virmati's feelings and emotions. The female gender is always expected to perform womanly duties, the roles of being a good daughter, wife and mother. The female protagonists of the novels are told by their mothers to learn the skills of being a good daughter and wife in the family. Virmati, Astha, Nisha, Nina and Shagun are all given suitable guidance about their roles in family and marital life. Mothers represent the symbol of tradition, culture and try to establish these virtues to their daughters. Mothers in patriarchal society condition their girl child at the young age to adapt and adopt the norms set up in the existing society. This creates a rift between the mother and the daughter because one imposes and the younger generation opposes. This conflict between the two causes maternal alienation. Maternal indifference, lack of support, sympathetic approach and concern for the girl child within the family system affect harmonious existence and hence most women characters search for love and bonding outside the family. Hence, family also becomes a site for oppression.

The younger generation women are initially traditional and passive but later understand their needs and aspirations. They do not blindly adhere to what their mothers teach them; instead, they revolt and ask questions about blind faith. They protest within the family set ups for autonomy and be part of social activism and raise their voice. Kapur makes her women characters participate in outside agenda as social activists and at home to rebel and raise voice against patriarchy.

Gender discrimination sweeps in the psyche of the family when the woman is bearing a child. Lot of care, attention and celebration happen to welcome the new born. Everyone in the family anticipates it to be son. This mind set is shown in all of Kapur's fiction. Family members of each of these protagonists honestly expect the arrival of the male baby. Kapur critiques this situation by indicating that even educated and NRI like Hemant in *A Married Woman* cannot erase this mindset.

One noteworthy aspect noted in Kapur's fiction is that older women are authoritative and impose power on the younger ones. There is power struggle within the family threshold. In this situation, most often, the male members especially the father figures are supportive of their daughters. Father figures in Kapur's fiction are supportive of daughter's education. They encourage them. Virmati's father, Astha's, and Nisha's father understand that education provides not only better match in marriages but also gives them economic independence. Kapur has not only shown how women are being exploited in a patriarchal society, by rigid laws and customs, socialisation of gender ethos but she has also pointed how women are subject to subordination by women themselves who may be mothers, mother-in-law or sisters. Virmati, Astha and Sona seek their father's support in educating themselves and having a career of their own. Father figures are not shown as oppressive agents where as women in family circles become the forces for domination. Father figures do have concern for their daughters to get married and be settled in life but they have much more liberal views. Kapur seems to suggest that patriarchal structure is not to be always blamed but women should have concern for other women. Women should not be blind upholders of patriarchy and tradition, but should have a sensible and empathetic approach towards other women.

Kapur's women protagonist like Virmati, Astha, Nisha and Shagun do protest patriarchal power structures which they encounter within family and also outside. They devise their own ways to resist and assert their individuality. They seek support from father figures and brush aside practices that dominate women. Kapur's women characters have learnt to identify their weakness and work towards shaping their identity by discarding patriarchal hegemony.

Each of the titles of Kapur's fiction are reservoirs of meaning. The titles act as symbols and metaphors. Titles are themselves signifiers. *Difficult Daughters* signify daughters who go against tradition and patriarchy and want to lead life in their own way. The spaces they create for themselves makes situation difficult for others and also for themselves. It is always easy to follow the regular path but if this is challenged, one becomes 'difficult' for everyone. All the titles of Kapur's fiction leave space for multiple meanings to interpret. Each title becomes a signifier of some other signifiers. The author, no doubt, has a deconstructive approach. She distorts, subverts and questions some practices. Thus, the titles *Difficult Daughters, Home, A Married Woman* do not signify one aspect but point to different signifiers. *Home* signifies warmth, tenderness and comfort. But for Nisha home becomes traumatic affair. Home also suggests the connectivity between women and domestic chores. Women are primarily associated with the idea of home. It is said women can build and also destruct the qualities of home. *A Married Woman* gives the idea of tradition, custom and heterosexual relation between two partners. This perception is dismantled in the very text. What the title signifies and what the text carries with it are different.

Kapur has skillfully shown the various social problems confronted by men, women and children as well. The problem of infertility and the preference for the male child in the family is a recurrent theme. In the families of Virmati, Astha, Nisha, Nina and Shagun, marriage plays a vital role and the family members eagerly await for a son. But the women protagonists have no particular interest for a male child. It is only the family members who infuse such thoughts in their daughters. Once again, Kapur shows how family becomes an oppressive mechanism and affect the psyche of the female members. When a couple is not able to bear children, it is most often the women who fall prey to insults and humiliations. Motherhood is highly glorified in the Indian context. Society expects a woman to get married at the right time and produce children. At the childhood stage itself, girl children are given messages about this. Therefore, infertility brings in a devastating effect on the lives of young women. Ida in *Difficult Daughters,* Sona and Rupa in *Home*, Nina in *The Immigrant*, Ishita in *Custody* become victims of these societal demands and at times they lose their mental balance. The idea of infertility is one most common problem these days and Kapur has taken this issue in most of her fiction. But Kapur's women are not meek, submissive and pessimistic. Sona's persistent prayers and hope make her dreams come true after ten years. Ida, Nina, Rupa and Ishita are optimistic and look for new directions where they can find fulfillment. They understand that motherhood is not the only fulfilling factor in their life. Ida and Nina look for new ventures for a meaningful existence, for Rupa, it is the pickle business that gives her success and happiness. Ishita who is most tortured for her infertility, fulfils her life by serving the orphan children, working for an NGO and also adopting Raman's daughter as her own. These women devise ways for meaningful existence and find happiness in their new ventures. Unlike some of the characters of Markandaya or Desai, they do not compromise or become neurotic, but they establish and seek happiness in their success, not just in the attainment of motherhood.

Another problem which the author has brought to the limelight is the matter of dowry. Sona, Sona's sister-in-law, Ishita are all condemned by their family members especially their mother-in-laws for bringing insufficient dowry. The texts suggest that men also become victims of patriarchy and tradition, although women are larger victims. Harish, Hemant and Raman suffer from patriarchal pressures. They cannot perform accordingly to their choices; they refrain from doing what seems correct because of societal and traditional demands. Because of this, characters suffer from alienation, loneliness, psychological turmoil and conflicts. The inner and external conflicts disturb the psyche of these characters. Virmati, Astha, Nisha and Nina feel alienated in their own homes. The psychological gets manifested in the form of frequent headaches and skin diseases which most characters suffer. The internal disturbances appear in the form of these health conditions. Astha and Shagun suffer severe headaches while for Nisha, it is the skin problem. Although Harish and Astha have proper family with children, yet they feel the presence of some lacuna in their lives and hence find themselves lonely and isolated. Kapur seems to address that much of the gaps that distances husband-wife is lack of communication. Harish, Hemant, Ananda, Raman do not speak up to their wives. They remain confined to their roles as husband and are engrossed in their own world that they find difficult to articulate their thoughts, feeling to their wives. Proper exchange of communication is lacking in the husband-wife relationship which gives rise to marital discords. Kapur suggests that in a marital relation, both man and the woman should open up and exchange thoughts. It should be not handled with a sense of duty consciousness.

Kapur's concern is not only for women but also for men and children. The problem of child sexual abuse is discussed through an incident that Nisha faces in her childhood. Arundhati Roy in her *The God of Small Things* also brings in this serious issue. Children are vulnerable at the hands of young adults, adults and sometimes male children themselves as in case of *Home* where a child abuses another child. Many women novelists concentrate only on the aspects related to women in particular. But Kapur has significantly broadened her thematic concerns. She discusses the problems faced by men, women and children as well. The traumatised mind of the child which became prey to sexual abuse is given a detailed account. Because of the horrific incident, the child's home itself becomes a nightmare for her and she wishes to go out of the home environment. "Three years have passed since her removal to her aunt's house, and the dark thing inside her is deeply buried" (*Home* 81).

Children's suffering and their psyche at the hands of divorced parents are well portrayed in her novel *Custody.* Most of her novels are in the form of bildungsroman which gives the author the scope to narrate the lives from the childhood stage. This form clearly gives the reader how the upbringing is shaped by the society, environment, and family and tradition right from birth. This form aptly suits to bring in the different clashes and conflicts that are represented. Conflicts between self/individuality and society, emotion and rationality, desire vs. commitment, conflicts between the mother and daughter and the dichotomy between tradition and modernity and the consequent impact on social values and ethics is well portrayed in Kapur's works.

Manju Kapur has also consistently explored the issue of identity in her novels. Her novels offer interesting ways of understanding the problematics of identity. Kapur explores the multiple ways in which our identities are constructed and offers us critical insight into multidimensionality of identity. Kapur seems to articulate that identity is a matter of conscious choice. Identity is fragmentary resulting in hybrid identities. Identity itself is a signifier, signifying so many identities and thus resulting in an ongoing and never-ending process, open ended rather than fixed and closed entity. In *Difficult Daughters*, Kapur talks about national identity and the identity yearned by women. Identity becomes a heavily constructed discourse. One of the important aspects of identity is that it needs to be continuously negotiated. Nina in *The Immigrant* for example has to negotiate with the markers of Indian identity be it food or dress and consciously adopt to situations based on need. So, the markers of Indian identity are also subject to change especially for the diaspora population. In a diasporic existence, displacement offers newer understanding of the concept of identity. Kapur's fictional works in some or other way problematise the very idea of identity and while doing so, does not arrive at or provide any concrete solution. They are left open ended to suggest that we must assimilate what seems proper and correct to one's mind and not stick to anything blindly. Kapur like other postmodern writers deconstructs the idea of identity. She explores national identity, identity of women, sexual identity, cultural identity and the diaspora identity. In fact, the term Indian English writing itself became a much debatable topic questioning the authenticity in portraying Indianess or the Indian identity. Postcolonial discourses treat identity as a continuous process which means it is subject to change.

Interestingly, it is only in her novel, *The Immigrant*, she brings to surface the various forces that make Indians to migrate, the consequences, and the gradual acceptance and the willingness to adapt and adopt for convenience in a globalised world. The reality presented is that these days, migration cannot be related to exile because that kind of life is consciously chosen, either for better prospects or personal commitments. Hence, the sense of alienation, cultural conflict, and isolation is already anticipated and painfully undertaken and more often the character is seen as assimilating a hybrid culture and identity. In this discourse, Kapur questions and deconstructs the very notion of identity, as there is nothing as 'one concrete identity' and that the identity that we speak about is subject to change. Kapur's characters, especially the women protagonist realise selfhood as freedom, choice, rights, equality, rationality and control of one's self. Her protagonists are poised between submission and resistance, passivity and action. The very instability of this subject contains within it the possibility of initiating a change.

Thus, Manju Kapur shows how transmigrants moving across different cultures and locations are caught physically and psychologically between two worlds. The displacement that we talk of is only geographical, and cultural but also spiritual. The love for privacy and independence as advocated by westerners are gradually imbibed by the immigrants. The theme of displacement and cultural identity is predominant here.

This probe into the text, gives an idea that in some way, Manju Kapur intends to deconstruct the concept of "indianess" as watertight category and calling into question anything related to it. There seems to be an attempt to deconstruct east/west binary oppositions. All that we think and do is as per our mental makeup. Nothing remains as permanent or fixed. Towards the end, we find Nina, the protagonist heading towards new territories with a carefree vision. The text comes to an end in the literal sense but it is only a fresh beginning. This is echoed through Nina who is proceeding to newer territories to venture.

Kapur's fiction are clearly Indian fiction as they represent the Indian identity. Kapur's texts have Indian names, ample usage of food imagery, the settings and locale, the Indianised usage of the English language, idioms and phrases common in India are all elaborately used. So, at once it becomes a text where an Indian reader can attach himself to. For a non-Indian reader, the text itself becomes a cultural signifier as literature is byproduct of a particular culture. But this cultural identity where we associate ourselves is also subject to fragmentation or change. Kapur's works question the authentication of these cultural markers. Kapur's women Virmati, Astha, Nisha, Nina, Shagun and Ishita all strive for self-identity. In this struggle for individuality, they are caught between values, traditions, ethics and societal pressures, yet they are bold enough to resist and emerge strongly to fight in order to achieve freedom of expression and thought.

The fixity of gendered and sexual categories is challenged. What we call sexual identity is ruptured and, in this case, the term 'a married woman' signifies some other signifiers. Here a married woman is not just associated with husband and family but also the outer world where she participates as a social activist and goes beyond boundaries to fulfill her suppressed desires. *A Married Woman*, as a text subverts the literary tradition of considering these subjects from a negative aspect. In this sense, the text becomes a postcolonial text that attempts to resist the cultural hegemony of colonial/nationalist discourse. The ideal of "womanhood", in this case a married woman, as conceived in the patriarchal society is subverted. The text is a bold attempt to give space and voice to these minorities in the public domain. Although Kapur does not advocate or moralise anything, there is a clear indication of emergence of lesbian identity. Kapur reiterates the notion where identity is a matter of conscious choice. Instead of fixed identity, we have now hybrid identities. Identity formation is never ending and is open ended rather than fixed and closed. So is Nina's life in *The Immigrant* which reinforces what the author intends to address.

Kapur subtly deconstructs some relationships within the family system. Motherhood is celebrated and myths about mother as dignified figure, the selfless, starving one who feeds the rest of the family and is the last to eat the remains, were celebrated and portrayed in most fiction, early and the present. But Kapur attempts to subvert this conventional image of motherhood. Kasturi in *Difficult Daughters* uses all methods and resorts to the use of twig for elimination of god's blessing 'the will of God' (9) from her body. Kasturi, although having a very traditional mind set and submits herself to patriarchy is forced by the situations to go against the norms of society.

The concept of motherhood is again subverted in *Custody*, where the children are at stake and we have the heroine plunging into the arms of another man for her personal needs. Mother, usually, is seen as a role model. But in *Difficult Daughters*, Ida pronounces, "the one thing I had wanted was not to be like my mother". The mother-daughter relationship is usually supposed to be empathetic, compassionate and friendly approach between the two. But this approach takes a different turn in Kapur's fiction. The concept of motherhood is challenged. The concept of motherhood is questioned when in *Home*, Kapur juxtaposes two sisters – Sona and Rupa, both of whom are unable to conceive even after years of marriage. But Sona is anxious and too concerned about the matter; whereas Rupa is much easy with it. Mothers often become the agents of patriarchal values. Daughters, on the other hand, resist this patriarchy, thus calling into question the smooth relation between mothers and daughters and also the power politics of elder women on the younger ones.

Women are stereotyped and subordinated in the roles assigned to them and are subject to male violence. Kapur's fiction explores the identities of women with respect to the roles assigned to them:

wife, mother, daughter that are conditioned by not only class and education but rooted in Indian mind set. Kapur's novels portray the plurality of female experiences and how each woman adopts different strategies for self-assertion and constructive growth.

Kapur does not point out a single or specific solution but shows how certain things remain arbitrary and a balanced, rational, positive approach can make lives better. Kapur's protagonists are young, educated and married. They come across different barriers at various thresholds of life. They face problems at parents as well as marital home. Against all odds, they reconstruct their lives and resolve their crisis. Kamala Markandaya's protagonists resolve their situation with reconciliation with society and self. Anita Desai's women cannot sustain life in such circumstances and turn out to be neurotic and submit to fate and disaster. Shoba De's women suffer from moral deterioration. Whereas Kapur's women face life with hope, confidence and emerge transformed and empowered. They resolve and rejuvenate themselves for the positive aspect. All the female protagonists initially long for love and attention but as they mature they participate in the world outside the home, become social activist or be part of freedom movement and so on. These women realise that there is more than being just a mother, wife and daughter. This self-realisation makes them to seek autonomy and space for themselves. But at times because of their upbringing or parental or societal pressure they tend to compromise to sustain marital harmony and stable life. The ordeals faced by women get manifested in the form of headaches or skin diseases that most of her women suffer from. But instead of settling in the parental home after a marital discord, they challenge life and make bold attempts. They raise their opinions, seek free expression of thoughts and choose to make their lives more meaningful. Even though at times Kapur's women make compromises for the sake of family or society, they evolve in an optimistic way. As a postmodern writer, Kapur speaks for women who should be assertive, bold and rational. Through Astha, Kapur voices:

> A woman should be self-controlled, strong willed, self-reliant and rational, having faith in the inner strength of womanhood. A

> meaningful change can be brought only from within by being free in the deeper psychic sense (AMarriedWoman 6).

Manju Kapur fiction also point out the fractured nature of the concept of identity. Kapur's works does explore the multifarious nature of identity and its formation in the contemporary times. The issue of identity has been an important thematic concern for Indian English writings. Identities are constructive in nature. Multidimensionality of identity is her desire to explore. Kapur problematises the issue of identity. The notion of identity should not be read as water tight compartments. Identities are negotiable, readjustable and fluid.

Virmati in *Difficult Daughters* wants the professor to marry her and give her a status in society. But after gaining the much-wanted identity of being the professor's second wife, she has to struggle within the family to sustain it. She faces other problems as well. Women in her fiction yearn for self-identity, but in struggling to achieve that, lose other things. Ananda in *The Immigrant* chooses to be called in westernised name – Andy. Nina, his wife has to transform herself to adapt to the new place. Their Indian identity is called into question in their diasporic life. The concept of having a single identity is itself dismantled.

Kapur like Chaucer or Dickens is a social chronicler. Her novels provoke serious thought to contemporary social issues that require attention. The thesis attempts to explore Kapur's views on the problematics of identity formation by an in-depth study of the responses of the characters in situations which call for assertion and reformulation of identity. Kapur's novels deconstruct the idea of fixed identity but project identity as flexible, fluid and muti-faceted. Kapur is interested in problematising the issue of identity rather than offering any straightforward or simplistic solution. She offers through her novels the complexities of such identities. Kapur's novels are open ended and not didactic and hence do not offer any quick or permanent solution. Her novels open up our minds to think, interrogate and shape our thinking. As a creative writer, she uses her literary art to raise various questions that surround us and thereby make us think to redefine our thoughts.

Kapur's novels are open ended and avoid fixed, closed happy ending. Every beginning leads to end which is only again a beginning. With this idea, *Difficult Daughters* begins with a funeral scene. It seems from every end, there is a new beginning.

Her novels are a literary expression for social change in thought and attitude. Certain myths, ideas are subverted and deconstructed. The idea of gender and its performative tasks, and motherhood are deconstructed. She reinforces the concept that gender is socially constructed and we perform accordingly. The idea of Motherhood is deconstructed. The image of mother stands high and this is deconstructed. Mothers are also to some extent act as oppressive forces on their daughters to mould them to patriarchal threshold. Identity and selfhood are not natural but are constructed consciousness. Deconstruction of patriarchal norms in tradition bound society is well achieved by her bold women characters. Heterosexuality is dismantled and all fixed notions of identity are subverted. Kapur subverts and breaks the canon by divulging in new perceptions. In this sense, she is a true postcolonial and postmodern writer. At the surface level, her novels seem to have a simple story line with straightforward narration but the thesis has attempted to bring in the underlying serious issues that the author addresses. Kapur through her novels rather than 'telling', 'shows' us. She gives a detailed picture of the lives of men and women around and voices for a balanced way of life which makes society more a better place. One thing common with all her texts is the idea of empowerment through education. She seems to hint that Education and economic independence are the two driving forces for women empowerment. Virmati understands that "It was useless in looking for answers inside the home. One had to look outside to education, freedom and the bright lights of Lahore colleges" (*Difficult Daughters* 15-16).

Her novels, no doubt, evoke female consciousness but at the same time it shows the concerns for the male gender as well. Kapur has a balanced approach to both the sexes and she looks at the various problems through an objective lens. Along with other postmodern writers like Shashi Deshpande, Gita Hariharan, Arundhati Roy, Anita Nair and Jaishree Misra, Manju Kapur has shown various modes of resistance to patriarchal norms. Gender roles and stereotypes are questioned and motherhood and identity has been redefined. Thematically, Kapur's fiction covers a wide platform. The lives of common man, man-woman relationship, infertility and divorce, gender discrimination, conflicts between traditional values and modern practices, east/west and cultural conflicts, problems faced in a diasporic existence and the issue of identity becomes the canvas of her fiction. Post modernism advocates multiplicity, pluralism, and open endedness. Kapur's novels sincerely portray the plurality of female experiences and how each woman adopts different strategies for self-assertion and constructive growth.

Kapur voices the fact that autonomy and economic independence can be achieved through education. Contemporary women writers like Kapur, through their texts, question the age-old traditions and patriarchal system and show signs of resistance to them. They re-represent women in their postmodern narratives. Hence, there are strong and bold women characters. They question the idea of 'being an ideal woman'. She critiques the patriarchal power structure of Hindu society through the characters. She deconstructs the notions of gender, equality and identity through the narrative. She has also pointed that however educated and forward notions, yet in Indian society, still the longing for a male child is prevalent. Kapur's novels refuse to supply any obvious, specific and direct viewpoints. Kapur believes in 'showing' instead of 'telling'. She would rather problematise than provide solutions. Her descriptive mode of narration combined with an objective outlook and open endings place her in the postmodern domain. Kapur does not point that education will eradicate all problems. In fact, Kapur's major women characters are well educated. She suggests that education will make us more rational and enable us to think more independently to solve our problems. Although already educated, some of the characters are shown to pursue higher studies. Kapur's novels clearly state the conviction that higher education and economic independence support women to take independent decisions. Her novels state that the lens of education and economic independence also helps to mitigate the threats of violence which women have to face in various relationships. Astha's father is liberated and believes that his daughter must study to expand her mental horizon.

Astha's father

> "...believes in the new. He feels that his daughter's future lay in her own hands, and these hands were to be strengthened by the number of books that passed through them" (*A Married Woman* 2).

Kapur's works gives us an impression of Kapur as a liberal and postmodern feminist. Liberal feminism advocates legal and political reforms and such an attainment is possible through woman's own actions, performances and reaction to situations. Women must assert their ability to achieve equality. Postmodern feminism dismantles binary divisions between sex and gender and that gender is only socially constructed. It believes women have different problems and the diversity of women is addressed. Hence, there cannot be single solution to all the problems. It criticizes stereotypical gender roles and believes in social change through realisation, awareness and rationality of thoughts. Kapur writes with these perspectives.

Kapur's excellence as a writer can be traced through her vision that looks at society from multiple perspectives and leaves an impact on the readers to redefine thought processes without offering any facile solution to the complexities of life. Kapur's works are written with a purpose to sensitise the society and bring in a social change for a better living. And for women, it is through education and economic independence. Kapur's works not only broaden our mental horizon but offer interesting literary studies especially through the postmodern lens. The texts leave gaps for multiple interpretations and analysis. As readers, we enjoy the story line and as literary scholars, peal the layers of meaning through theoretical analysis of the polemics of gender, identity, sexuality and other artifacts initiated by postmodern thinkers.

Works Cited

Primary Sources

Kapur, Manju. *Difficult Daughters*. London. Faber and Faber, 1998. Print.

---, *A Married Woman*. London. Faber and Faber, 2003. Print.

---, *Home*. London. Random House Ltd, 2006. Print.

---, *The Immigrant*. Random House India, 2008. Print.

---,*Custody*. Random House India, 2011. Print.

Secondary Sources

Books

Andermahr, Sonya. *A Glossary of Feminist Theory*. London: Arnold Publishers, 2002 Print.

Bande, Usha. *Writing Resistance: A Comparative Study of the Selected Novels by Women Writers.* Shimla: Indian Institute of Advanced Studies, 2006. Print.

Bandyopadhyay, Sumana. *Indianisation of English: Analysis of Linguistic Features in Selected Post-1980 Indian English fiction*. Ph. D thesis. Kanpur: IIT Kanpur. 2007

Beauvoir, Simone de. *The Second Sex.* Trans. And ed. H.H. Parsley. London: Picador Classics Books, 1988. Print.

Berger, Peter L. and Brigitte Berger. *Sociology: A Biographical Approach.* 1972. USA: Basic Books; England: Penguin Book, 1976. Print.

Bhabha.K. Homi. *The Location of Culture.* London. Routledge, 1994. Print.

Bhatnagar K.C. *Realism in Major Indo English Fiction.* Bareilly: Prakash Book Depot, 1980. Print.

Bose, Brinda, ed. "Introduction." *Translating Desire: The Politics of Gender and Culture in India*. New Delhi: Katha, 2002. Print.

Butler, Judith. *Gender Trouble; Feminism and the Subversion of Identity.* New York: Routledge 1999. Print.

Chakraborthy, Krishna. *Family in India*. Jaipur and New Delhi: Rawat Publications, 2002. Print.

Choudhuri, Sucheta Mallick. *Transgressive territories: queer space in Indian Fiction and Film*. Ph. D thesis, University of Iowa. 2009. Print.

Clara, Nubile. *The Danger of Gender Caste Class and Gender in Contemporary Indian Women's Writing*. New Delhi: Sarup Book Publishers Pvt. Ltd., 2003. Print.

Das, Bijay Kumar. *Postmodern Indian English literature.* Atlantic Publishers, 2003. Print.

Dass, Veena Noble. *Feminism and Literature.* New Delhi: Prestige Books, 2009. Print.

Deshpande, Shashi. *Writing from the Margin and Other Essays*. New Delhi: Penguin India, 2003. Print.

Dhawan, R.K. *Essays on the New Literatures*. New Delhi: Prestige Books, 2003. Print.

.... *Feminism and Recent Indian Literature Vol 2.* New Delhi: Prestige Books, 2009. Print.

.... *Indian Women Writers.* New Delhi: Prestige Books, 2001. Print.

.... *Indian Writing in the* New *Millennium.* New Delhi: Indian Association for English Studies, 2000. Print.

Forster, E.M. *Aspects of Novel*. London: Penguin Books, 1979. Print.

Foucault, Michel. *The History of Sexuality*. Vol.1. London: Penguin Books, 1978. Print.

Friedan, Betty. *The Feminine Mystique*. London: Penguin, 1992. Print.

Jain, Jasbir. *Writing Women Across Cultures*. Jaipur: Rawat Publications, 2002. Print.

Jandial, Gur Pyari. *Evolving a Feminist Tradition: The Novels of Shashi Deshpande and Manju Kapur*. Delhi: Awaiting Publication, 2003. Print.

Jha, Uma Shankar and Premlata Pujari. *Indian Women Today: Tradition, Modernity and Challenge*. New Delhi: Kanishka Publishers, 1996.Print.

Kapoor, Promilla. *The Changing Status of the Working Women of India.* Delhi: Vikas Publishing House Private Ltd, 1975. Print.

Kaur, Iqbal. *Gender and Literature*. Delhi: B.R. Publishing Corporation, 1992. Print.

Klages, Mary. *Literary theory: A Guide for the Perplexed*. London: Continuum Books, 2006. Print.

Kripal, Viney. *The Postmodern Indian Novel in English.* New Delhi: Allied Publishers, 1996. Print.

K.R. Srinivasa Iyengar, *Indian Writing in English*. New Delhi: Sterling Publishers, 1983.

Kumar, Ashok. *The Novels of Manju Kapur: A Feministic Study*. New Delhi: Sarup, 2010. Print.

Kumar, Gajendra. *Indian English Literature: A New Perspective*. New Delhi: Sarup and Sons, 2001. Print.

Meenakshi Mukherjee. *The Twice Born Fiction: Themes and Techniques of the Indian Novel in English*. New Delhi: Arnold-Heinemann, 1971. Print.

.... Mukherjee, *Realism and Reality:The Novel and Society in India*, New Delhi: Oxford Univ. Press, 1985. Print.

Millett, Kate. *Sexual Politics*. New York: Double Day, 1970. Print.

Mill, J.S. *The Subjection of Women.* London: J.M. and Sons Ltd., 1982. Print.

Naik.M. K: *Perspectives on Indian Fiction in English*, Abhinav Publications, New Delhi 1985. Print.

Naik, M. K. and Shyamala A. Narayan. *Indian English Literature 1980-2000. A critical Survey*. New Delhi: Pencraft International, 2001. Print.

Nitonde, Rohidas. *In Search of a Feminist Writer.* Bloomington: Partridge Publishing, 2014. Print

Nubile, Clara. *The Danger of Gender*. New Delhi: Sarup. 2003. Print.

Prasad, Amar Nath. *New Lights on Indian Woman Novelists in English Vol.4.* New Delhi: Sarup and Sons, 2008. Print.

Rajan, Sunder Rajeswari. *Signposts: Gender Issues in Post-Independence India*. New Delhi: Kali for Women, 1999. Print.

.... *Real and Imagined Women: Gender, Culture and Postcolonialsim*. London and New York: Routledge, 1993.

Rajput, Kalpna. *Remapping the Female Map: Jhumpa Lahiri and Manju Kapur.* New Delhi: Yking Books, 2012. Print.

Ray, Mohit and Kundu, Rama. *Studies in Woman Writers in English Vol. IV.* New Delhi: Atlantic Publishers and Distributors, 2005. Print.

Robert B. Henkle, *Reading the Novel: An Introduction to the Techniques of Interpreting Fiction.* New York: Harper& Row, 1977. Print.

Roy, Anuradha. *Patterns of Feminist Consciousness in Indian Women Writers.* New Delhi: Prestige Books, 1999. Print.

Said, Edward. *Orientalism: Westerns conceptions of the OrientIndian.* Penguin Books, 1978. Print.

Sharma, Ram. *Rise of New Women: Novels of Manju Kapur.* New Delhi: Manglam Publications, 2013. Print.

Singh, Sushila. *Feminism and Recent Fictions in English.* New Delhi: Prestige Books, 2013. Print.

.... *Feminism: Theory, Criticism and Analysis.* New Delhi: Pencraft International, 1997. Print.

Sinha, Sunita. *Post-colonial women writers New Perspectives.* Atlantic publishers, 2008. Print.

Sree, S. Prasanna. *Psycho Dynamics of Women in the Postmodern Literature.* New Delhi: Sarup and Sons, 2008. Print.

Tharu, Susie and K. Lalita, ed. *Women Writing in India: 600 B.C to the Twentieth Century.* 2 vol. s New Delhi: Oxford University Press, 1993, 1999. Print.

Vanita, Ruth and Saleem Kidwai. ed *Same-sex love in India: Readings from Literature and History.* New York: Palgrave, 2001. Print.

Wollstonecraft, Mary. *A Vindication of the Rights of Woman.* New Delhi: Deep and Deep publications, 1992. Print.

Woolf, Virginia. *A Room of One's Own.* Ed. Jennifer Smith. Cambridge: Cambridge University Press, 2001. Print.

Articles in Books & Journals

Ahmad, Nadia. "Cracking India: Tradition versus Modernity in AttiaHosain'sSunlightona Broken Column and Manju Kapur's Difficult Daughters." *The Road to Baghdad, or Traveling Biculturalism: Theorising a Bicultural Approach to Contemporary World Fiction.* Ed. GönulPultar. Washington: New Academia, 2005. 199-218.Print.

Alterno, Letizia. "Shreds of Indianness: Identity and Representation in Manju Kapur's The Immigrant."*Postliberalisation Indian Novels in English: Politics of Global Reception and Awards.* Ed. Aysha Iqbal Viswamohan. London: Anthem Press, 2013. 77-86. Print.

Azhar, Darkhasha. "Universal Angst of Modern Marriage: A Critique of Manju Kapur's Custody." *Cyber Literature* 31.2 (Dec 2013): 37-46. Print.

Balakrishnan, Anita. "Marriage, Tradition and Autonomy: The Quest for Self-discovery in Manju Kapur's *A Married Woman.*" *South Asian Review* (University of Pittsburgh), Vol. XXV, No. 2, (2004): 104-112. Print.

Bala, Suman and Subhash Chandra. "Manju Kapur's *Difficult Daughters*: An Absorbing Tale of Fact and Fiction."*50 Years of Indian Writing: A Commemorative Volume Highlighting the Achievement of Post-independence Indian Writing in English and Literature in Translation.* Ed. R.K. Dhawan. New Delhi: Prestige, 1999. 105-10. Print.

Banerjee, Laksmisree. "Indian Women's Voices: The Postcolonial and Post-Modernist Era." *Postcolonial Discourse: A Study of Contemporary Literature.* Ed. R.K. Dhawan. New Delhi: Prestige Books, 2000. 65-88. Print.

Bhatnagar, Monika. "Manju Kapur's Home: A Microcosm of Indian Family Institution." *The Vedic Path* 87.3 and 4 (Jul-Sep/Oct-Dec 2013): 86-94. Print.

Bhatt, Indira. "Marriage-The Summum Bonum Of Woman's Life: A Studyof Manju Kapur's *Difficult Daughters.*"*Indian Women Novelists in English.* Ed. Amar Nath Prasad. New Delhi: Atlantic Publishers, 2001. 111-124. Print.

Boehmer, Elleke. "'First realise your need': Manju Kapur's Erotic Nation." *Alternative Indias: Cultural Diversity in Contemporary Literature in English.* Ed. Peter Morey and Alex Tickell. Amsterdam: Rodopi, 2005. 53-70. Print.

Chanana, Kuhu. 'Plularity of Lesbian Existence in Modern Indian Writers: Manju Kapur, Rajkamal Chaudhary and Geetanjali Shree." *Indian Literature* 54.3-257 (May-Jun 2010): 190-219. Print.

Chakravarty, Joya. "A Study of *Difficult Daughters* and *A Married Woman.*" *Novels of Manju Kapur: A Feministic Study*. Ed. Ashok Kumar. New Delhi: Sarup, 2010. 53-62. Print.

.... "A Comparative Analysis of Arundhati Roy's *The God of Small Things* and Manju Kapur's *Difficult Daughters." Indian Writing in English: Perspectives.* Ed. Joya Chakravarty. New Delhi: Atlantic Publishers and Distributors, 2003. 93-100. Print.

Chotai, Nutan. "Changing Faces of Women in Manju Kapur's *Home.*" *Contemporary Fiction: An Anthology of Female Writers.* Ed. Vandana Pathak, Urmila Dabirand Shubha Mishra. New Delhi: Sarup, 2008. 127-134. Print.

Chaudhary, Sushila and Shashi Bansal. "Quest for Feminine Identity – a Reading of Manju Kapur's The Immigrant." *Comtemporary Vibes* 8.29 (Oct-Dec 2012): 22-24. Print.

Chauhan, Vibha S. "Women, History and Fiction: Kapur's *Difficult Daughters* and Baldwin's *What the Body Remembers." Desert in Bloom: Contemporary Indian Women's Fiction in English.* Ed. Meenakshi Bharat. New Delhi: Pencraft International, 2004.36-44.Print.

Choubey, Asha. "Mothers and Daughters: A Comparative Critique of Fasting, Feasting and Difficult Daughters." *Critical Responses to Anita Desai*: Vol-II. 2004. 283-293. Print.

Chowdhury, Anupama. "Exile at Home: A Woman's Quest for Identity in Manju Kapur's The Immigrant." *The Literary Criterion* 45.1 (2010): 29-42. Print

......., "Chunification of English: Techniques in the Novels of Manju Kapur" *Points of View* 18.2 (Win 2011): 100-106. Print.

......., "Exile at Home: A Woman's Quest for Identity in Manju Kapur's *The Immigrant". The Literary Criterion.* Vol. XLV No. I. (2010). 22-34. Print.

Chhikara, Mayur. "Manju Kapoor's *Difficult Daughters* – A Saga of Feminist Autonomy and Separate Identity." *Language in India* 10.7 (Jul. 2010): 188-95. Print.

Clarke, Cheryl. "Lesbianism, An Act of Resistance." *This Bridge Called My Back: Writing by Radical Women of Color.* Ed. Cherrie Moraga. New York: Women of Color Press, 1983. 99-117. Print.

Das Gupta, Monica et.al. "Why is Son Preference So Persistent in East and South Asia? A Cross-Country study of China, India and the Republic of Korea." *The Journal of Development Studies* Vol. 40, No.2, (Dec 2003): 153-187. Print.

Dhawan, R.K. "Introduction: Entering the New Millennium through Indian Writing" *Indian Writing in the New Millennium.* Ed. R.K. Dhawan. New Delhi. Chaman Offset Press, 2000. 9-22. Print.

Dwivedi, A.N. "Manju Kapur's*Home:* A Feminist Reading." *Novels of Manju Kapur: AFeministic Study.* Ed. Ashok Kumar. New Delhi: Sarup, 2010. 38-45. Print.

Dwivedi, O.P. "The Glorification of 'The Second Sex': A Quest for Female Consciousness in Manju Kapur's*Difficult Daughters.*" *Novels of Manju Kapur: A FeministicStudy.* Ed. Ashok Kumar. New Delhi: Sarup, 2010. 31-37. Print.

Jain, Jasbir. "Towards the 21st Century: The Writing of the 1990s." *Indian Writing in English: The Last Decade.* Ed. Rajul Bhargava. Jaipur: Rawat Publications, 2002. 11-25. Print.

.... "Positioning the 'Post' in Post-Feminism: Reworking of Strategies". *Indian Feminism.* Eds. Jasbir Jain, Avadhesh Kumar Singh. New Delhi: Creative Books, 2001. Print.

.... "Daughters of Mother India in Search of a Nation: Women's Narrative about The Nation." *Economic and Political Weekly* Vol.41, No.17, (April 2006): 1654-1660. Print.

Jandial, Gur Pyari. "Evolving a Feminist Tradition: The Novels of Shashi Deshpande and Manju Kapur." *The Atlantic Literary Review* 4.3 (Jul.-Sept. 2003): 108-128. Print.

........"Manju Kapur's Difficult Daughters: A Study in Transition from Chaos to Integration." *The Commonwealth Review* 12.1(2000-2001): 93-100. Print.

Jha, Ira. "Manju Kapur's The Immigrant: an ode to woman's psyche." *Cyber Literature* 23.1 (Jun 2009): 73-85. Print.

Jha, Surendra Narayan. "The Treatment of Modern Women in Indian English Novel and Manju Kapur's Difficult Daughters." *Reflections on Indian English Literature*: (2002): 210-226. Print.

Juneja, Anita. "The Predicament of Indian Women in Difficult Daughters". *Poetcrit.* XX.2 (Jul. 2007): 60-70. Print.

Kalpagam, U. "Life Experiences, Resistance and Feminist Consciousness." *Indian Journal of Gender Studies* Vol. 7, No.2, (2000): 167-184. Print.

Kumar, Satendra. "Manju Kapur's Difficult Daughters: a Semio-Cultural Analysis." *The Atlantic Literary Review Quarterly* 11.4 (Oct-Dec 2010): 88-101.Print.

Malik, Seema. "Crossing Patriarchal Threshold: Glimpses of the Incipient New Woman in Manju Kapoor's Difficult Daughters." *Indian Women Writers* Ed. R. K. Dhawan, New Delhi: Prestige Books (2001):132-137. Print.

Manohar, D. Murali. "Women's Empowerment via Job/Career in Some Indian English Women's Novels." *Poetcrit* 21.1 (Jan 2008): 5-11. Print.

Mishra, Sudesh. *"From Sugar to Masala: Writing by the Indian Diaspora"* An Illustrated History of Indian Literature in English, Ed. Arvind Krishna Mehrotra, New Delhi: Permanent Black (2003) 45-61. Print.

Nayak, Bhagabat. "Love and Longing in Manju Kapur's Difficult Daughters." *Indian English Literature*: Vol. III. (2000): 156-165. Print.

Phogat, Geeta and Kiran Sikka. "Breaking Stereotypes: a feminist perspective of Manju Kapur's Novels." *The Atlantic Literary Review Quarterly* 13.2 (Apr-Jun 2012): 61-67. Print

Rastogi, Pallavi. "Manju Kapur." *South Asian Novelist in English: An A – Z Guide.* (2003): 122-124. Print.

Rishi, Jaydeep. "Mother-Daughter in Manju Kapur's Difficult Daughters." *Indian English Novel in the Ninetees.* (2002): 90-95. Print.

Roy, Manju. "Readability of Manju Kapur's Difficult Daughters." *The Commonwealth Review* 12.1 (2000-2001): 62-69. Print.

.... "Language and Style in Manju Kapur's Difficult Daughters." *Indian Journal of Postcolonial Literatures* 10.1 (Jun 2010): 147-153. Print.

Saharan, Asha. "Body as an Ideological Site: representation of Female Bodies in Manju Kapur's Fiction." *Littcrit* 39.2 – 76 (Dec 2013): 87-92. Print.

Shanthi, S. "Treatment of Women in Manju Kapur's Custody." *Trends in Kalis Research* 8.1 (Dec 2015): 73-76. Print.

Sharma, Pooja. "Manju Kapur's A Married Woman: deterritorialising Desire." *Samyukta*11.1 (Jan 2011):43-57. Print.

Shing, Veena. "How Difficult are Difficult Daughters? Sunlight on a Broken Column and Difficult Daughters as Female Bildungsroman." *Contemporary Indian Literature: Positions and Expositions* (2000): 161-175. Print.

Showalter, Elaine. "A Literature of Their Own: British Women Novelists from Bronte to Lessing." *Feminist Literary Theory*: A Reader, Ed. Mary Eagleton. 3rd ed. UK: Wiley Blackwell (2011).

Thoma, T.T. "The Quest for Fulfillment in Manju Kapur's Custody." *Indian Journal of Postcolonial Literatures* 13.2 (Dec 2013): 124-130. Print.

Verma, Daisy. "Tradition Versus Modernity in Difficult Daughters." *Journal of English Literature and Language* 4.1 (Jun 2010): 74-77. Print.

Warake, N.S. "Quest for Identity and Survival: a study of Manju Kapur's Home." *Journal of Literature, Culture and Media Studies* 2.4 (Jul-Dec 2010): 268-278. Print.

Reviews

Banerji, Jaya. "Complicated Lives." Rev. of *Difficult Daughters. Indian Review of Books 8.7* (16 Apr-15 May 1999): 6-7.

Basu, Chitralekha. "A Meeting of Minds." Rev. of *A Married Woman. The Times Literary Supplement* 5212 (February 21 2003):23.

Chakravarthy, Radha. Rev. of *Home. Indian Horizons* 53. (Sum 2006): 117-119.

Clements, Madeline. "Fractured Families." Rev. of Custody. The Times Literary Supplement 5634 (Mar 25 2011):21.

Kohil, Suresh. *Rev. of Home. Indian Literature* 50.4-234 (Jul-Aug 2006): 188-190.

Rollason, Christopher. "Not Exactly like Home." *Rev of The Immigrant. Seva Bharati Journal of English Studies* 5. (Feb 2009): 105-109.

Interviews

Farhad, J. Dadyburjor. *An Interview with Manju Kapur*. 22 Mar. 2006. <www. dnaindia.com/report.asp. ewsID=101 9404> Accessed October 20, 2014.

Pathak, Vandana. "Rendezvous with Manju Kapur". *Contemporary Fiction: An Anthology of Female Writers*. Ed. Vandana Pathak, Urmila Dabir and Shubha Mishra. New Delhi: Sarup and Sons, 2008. p.111-126.

Kapur, Manju, interviewed by Shana M. Verghis: "'I wasn't a writer, I was an academic'". *The Pioneer* 17 Jan. 2011.<www.dailypioneer.c

om/311063/%E2%80%98I-wasn%E2%80%99t-a-writer-I-was-an-academic%E2%80%99.html>.

Pande, Ira. *An Interview with Manju Kapur.* The Hindu, 5 Jan. 2003. <www.hinduonnet.com/thehindu/mag/2003/01/05/stories/2003010500-390300.htm> Accessed September 25. 2014.

Rajan, Anjana. *Seeds of Hope: An Interview with Manju Kapur*. The Hindu 5 Oct. 2008. < www.hindu.com/lr/2008/10/05/stories/2008100550160500.htm> Accessed February 18, 2010.

Singh, Jai Arjun. *An Interview with Manju Kapur*. Jabberwock website, 9 Aug. 2008.<http://jaiarjun.blogspot.com/2008_08_01_ archive.html> Accessed January 10th, 2014.

Verghis, Shana M. *An Interview with Manju Kapur*. The Pioneer 17 Jan. 2011. <www.dailypioneer.com/311063/%E2%80%98Iwasn%E2%80%99t-a-writer-I-was-an-academic%E2%80%99.html>Accessed June 14, 2014.

Index

F

G

H

I

J

K

L

M